MAKE
A LIVING
DESIGNING
LOGOS

BY IAN PAGET @LOGOGEEK

This book is independent and self-published.
I welcome your ideas and suggestions for
continuous improvement. Please don't hesitate
to email your feedback to ian@logogeek.com.
Your support is greatly appreciated!

Follow **@logogeek**

**FOR MY EVIE.
I HOPE THIS BOOK INSPIRES
YOU TO DREAM BIG & MAKE IT
HAPPEN, ONE STEP AT A TIME.**

Heart for Evie x

CONTENTS

YOUR TIME'S VALUABLE, SO
IF YOU WANT TO SKIP & READ
ONLY THE SECTIONS THAT
INTEREST YOU, GO FOR IT!

I WANT TO HELP YOU MAKE A LIVING DESIGNING LOGOS.

BUT THERE'S NOT JUST ONE WAY TO DO IT.

Every designer has a unique story to tell. Their creative process is personal, and they've established their own business processes and techniques to consistently find great clients.

That's why I didn't want to write a 'how to' book. Instead, I want to share my experience. That way, you can be confident that the tips and advice I share in this book actually work.

There are endless routes to success, and yours will be unique to you. I encourage you to continually learn from the experiences of others so that you can take the best lessons to adapt and improve your approach.

To help with that, this book is a companion to *The Logo Geek Podcast*, where I interview successful designers to discover how they've made a living designing logos. I also speak to entrepreneurs and marketing experts so that together we can learn valuable skills to thrive as a community.

In addition to the podcast, I've created *The Logo Geek Community*, where you can meet other designers who share your interests, ask questions, and receive the support you need to keep growing.

To listen to the podcast, head to:

LOGOGEEK.UK/PODCAST

To join the community, head to:

LOGOGEEK.UK/COMMUNITY

HOW I GOT INTO LOGO DESIGN

My design career started at a medical company. I had good art and design skills and was hired into the team creating posters, booklets and catalogues to support the national sales team. I had no formal design education or knowledge of the tools, so the designs I did initially were simple, like three-fold leaflets.

As I could draw well, I was asked if I could create a few product illustrations that would be used within "directions for use" documentation. I had never used the software previously, but I was able to figure out the tools with some guidance. To really understand them, I started working through tutorials in my own time, and as time passed, I started to get really good at creating accurate product illustrations. In the process, I was unknowingly mastering the software used to create logos.

In that role, I became the go-to person for design tasks, and that attracted my first logo design project. A colleague had sketched out a logo for her motorcycle club and asked if I could draw it up professionally. Being an eager and excited twenty-year-old, I quickly agreed and created the logo one evening for just £20.

I also started doing the occasional free logo for bands I found on MySpace, the most popular social platform at the time. Nothing I did back then was very good, however, I was having fun learning.

It wasn't until a few years later when I joined a web design agency that I ventured into the world of professional logo design. I secured a position as the company's first full-time UK based designer, responsible for tackling a wide range of design projects. While my proficiency with design tools had significantly improved by this point, I still felt like I was thrown into the deep end.

Fortunately, my passion for learning and my willingness to embrace challenges propelled me forward. I embraced any task that came my way, doing whatever it took to deliver results. Thanks to my dedication and hard work, I eventually earned a well-deserved promotion to the role of Design Director.

I primarily focused on designing websites in that position, although occasionally, a logo design project would come my way. I enjoyed the challenge; however, there were very few projects like it. I was eager to do more.

In my free time, I had recently finished working on a long-term personal project with friends. It was an iPhone game where I designed a long list of characters, backgrounds, maps and graphic elements. It was a fun project, and I'm proud of the work I did, but doing it along side a demanding Design Director role, with a long commute, meant I was working day and night to get things done. I was feeling tired and burned out.

Once the game was completed, I found myself at a crossroads. Initially, I decided to take a break from large personal design projects. Although, after a few weeks of much-needed rest, I suddenly found myself inspired, and a new creative endeavor landed on my lap.

I discussed my thoughts over dinner, and my love for logo design naturally surfaced. Despite having created only a handful of logos at that point, it struck me as the perfect project to sink my teeth into. Logo design was not only an enjoyable pursuit for me, but also an ideal one, as I could take on a project and see it through to completion within a few weeks.

The thought of diving deeper into logo design, honing my skills, and mastering them filled me with a hunger for knowledge and a burning desire to develop as a designer.

As a starting point, I created a website to showcase the logos I had already done. I needed a domain name, so I wrote down a list of potential business names. Almost everything was already taken from a list of over 100 ideas, and near the bottom of the list was "Logo Geek." Surprisingly, it was available, and I registered it immediately.

Little did I know that that moment would change my life forever. I started that website for fun, however, ten years later, I'm now in a position where I design logos for a living. I've won awards. I've been featured in books and magazines. I've been interviewed on some of the biggest design podcasts and websites. I've even been on the jury for several design awards. I host a podcast, and I've built a thriving community that helps me continue learning while also supporting other designers. My love and passion for logo design grows deeper each year, and I'm now making a decent living from it.

Although there was no intentional plan, I've been able to carve out a life for myself that circles around logo design, where I'm actively designing logos for companies around the world. I want to share how I achieved that and the lessons I've learned.

That's me, Ian Paget, standing by my ever-growing collection of design books

In this book, I share what makes a good logo, the tools I use, the processes I follow, how I present my logos, and how I deliver the final files. I also dive into how I've built a reputation as a logo designer, how I attract clients, and my approach for selling logos.

Mastering the art of logo design is a lifelong journey – it's a path I'm still on myself. To help you continue learning, at the back of this book, you'll find a list of books and resources that I recommend.

This isn't a set-in-stone formula for success. It's an overview of what's worked for me. The same thing may not work for you, however, I hope you'll take away a few lessons from my journey to apply to your own.

Whatever your personal goals, background or experience, I hope that by sharing my story, the processes I use and the lessons I've learned, will inspire you to fulfil your dream to make a living designing logos too.

Listen to the Podcast

THE LOGO GEEK PODCAST WITH IAN PAGET

Building a Reputation as a Logo

0:02 −31:19

Press hon

PART 1

ABOUT LOGOS

BEFORE MAKING A LIVING DESIGNING LOGOS, YOU'LL NEED TO KNOW HOW TO CREATE THEM. BEFORE YOU CAN DO THAT, THERE'S SOME STUFF I FEEL YOU SHOULD KNOW.

IN THIS SECTION, I'LL DISCUSS THE ROLE OF A LOGO, THE CHARACTERISTICS OF A SUCCESSFUL LOGO, & THE DIFFERENT TYPES OF LOGOS.

WHAT'S THE PURPOSE OF A LOGO?

The purpose of a logo is to identify a product, company or service. They're unique, like a signature or thumbprint.

Logos are everywhere we turn… look around you now, and you'll probably spot several.

Each logo, despite being simple, will conjure up feelings about the company it represents – its ads, jingles, marketing messages, products, and possibly even the people behind it.

Some logos might be important to you and be part of your identity. You might choose to wear clothing with a particular logo because it tells others what type of person you are, the type of films you watch, the music you listen to, the sports team you support, or the company you work for.

A logo doesn't operate in isolation. It's one small, but essential, part of a visual identity, and that identity represents a brand. As Sagi Haviv, partner and designer at Chermayeff & Geismar & Haviv, gracefully said, "A logo is the period at the end of a sentence, not the sentence itself."

There are many definitions of a brand. However, my favourite definition comes from Marty Neumeier, author of The Brand Gap, who says, "A brand is a person's gut feeling about a product, service or organisation."

A brand is something a business has no absolute control over. However, they can influence it with branding, which is the process of managing the experiences individuals have with a company, product or service.

Branding can influence all corners of a business, including positioning, product and more, and since you're reading this book, you're probably a graphic designer or want to be one. This means you will focus on designing the visual identity of a brand.

A visual identity includes many elements, such as fonts, colours, patterns, shapes, images, symbols, and logos. These elements all work together to help people identify which brand they want to purchase.

You see branding in action when you visit a supermarket. In every aisle, there are so many options to choose from. You gravitate to those you know and trust. The logo, along with the supporting identity, helps you differentiate one product from the other.

Despite all the work that goes into building a brand and its supporting visual identity, one thing rules them all. If only one image can represent the brand, it's the logo.

WHAT MAKES A GOOD LOGO?

If you design logos, you must understand what makes a good logo and why. Let's dive into the characteristics of what I believe makes for an effective logo.

IT'S VERSATILE

A well-designed logo is the face of the business. It needs to work effectively everywhere – in small sizes, such as social media icons, and large sizes, such as on a building exterior. It needs to work effectively on a website, vehicles, packaging, products, uniforms… the list goes on. It also needs to work in colour, in black and white, and when placed over an image or a background colour.

With so much flexibility required, you'll never have just one version of a logo. You'll have variations for different situations. Versions for print and digital uses. Versions in full colour, black and white, and maybe even variants for small and large use too.

To ensure a logo is versatile, some designers will argue that a logo should first be designed in solid black. While I agree with this and feel it's good practice, I believe that as long as a separate solid colour variant can be created, there's no need to add restrictions to your creativity.

IT'S SIMPLE

If a logo is simple, it works everywhere.

A simple logo is easy to remember and identify when you see it again. A busy logo, in comparison, will make identification more difficult.

If something doesn't need to be there when designing a logo, remove it. If the logo contains multiple ideas, keep the strongest and remove the others.

Simple doesn't mean that the design should be minimal, though. It means that it should use the lowest possible number of elements necessary to get across the desired look and feel.

IT'S LEGIBLE

If you can't clearly work out what the company is called by looking at the logo, there's a problem with the design.

It's common to see logos where one of the letters has been styled to look like something else. Unless the word remains clearly legible, I would avoid this.

When you work in isolation, you can miss the obvious, so if you need clarification, share the design with a friend. If there's any doubt at all, revise the design. It can be a costly mistake for your client if their customers cannot work out the company name.

The book I'm posing with here is Trade Marks & Symbols Volume 1 by Yasaburo Kuwayama

IT'S DISTINCT & MEMORABLE

Since the role of a logo is to identify, it needs to be sufficiently distinct to be recognised. It should be memorable and different enough to persist in our minds. To do this effectively, you'll need to consider the competitive landscape in which the logo will be seen and compared with others. If you understand this, you can identify ways to stand out from the competition.

IT DIFFERENTIATES

When a logo is placed alongside its competitor's logos, you need to be able to distinguish one business from another. This simply means that the logos should look different in some way. Colour is often an easy way to do this, but shape and form can achieve this too.

IT'S APPROPRIATE

While a logo should look different from its competitors, the overall aesthetic and feel should remain appropriate for the business. For example, bold, bouncy, bright fonts easily allow an accounting firm to stand out from its competitors; however, doing so wouldn't be appropriate. It would look unprofessional for a business dealing with finances.

IT LOOKS TO THE FUTURE

A logo shouldn't be designed solely to reflect what the company is like today. You should also consider where it plans to be in the future. For example, if a company sells shoes today and its logo contains a shoe, it would become problematic if they ever wanted to expand their product offering.

This was what Adidas did when it first started out in 1949. Its first logo featured a shoe, and twenty-two years later, it changed to use the three stripes we know today. Not only is this more distinctive and versatile, it also allows the business to grow in any direction it desires.

IT'S WELL-EXECUTED

You can have a great idea, but if the final logo is poorly executed, it will reflect poorly on the business. Quality of execution ultimately comes with experience. To help you with this, I share advice for constructing a logo effectively later in this book (page 74).

Even when you understand what makes a good logo, every scenario will present different challenges. Your client's unique business goals will determine where and how their logo will be used, so you may find that you need to "break the rules" occasionally. However, in most cases, if you design logos that fulfil all these "rules," you'll soon be designing excellent logos.

TYPES OF LOGOS

There are a few different types of logos that you may work on. I've broken this down into six categories, which we'll now discuss.

SYMBOLS

When people think of a logo, they'll probably picture a Symbol, such as the Apple logo, the Nike swoosh, the greatly missed Twitter bird, or the Starbucks Siren.

Symbols can be either pictorial or abstract.

Alongside the Symbol, there's usually a supporting wordmark displaying the company's name, however, a Symbol is often used on its own too.

ADVANTAGES

- You can create multiple configurations, known as lockups, allowing for greater flexibility.

- Symbols work more effectively at smaller sizes than typography-based designs.

- Symbols cross the language barrier, allowing the same consistent image to be used globally.

DISADVANTAGES

When you first see a typography-based design, you'll immediately know the business name. However, a new symbol will be meaningless until it's been seen repeatedly. That means that if you want the brand to be recognised by a symbol, in the way that Nike are, it can be a very costly and time-consuming pursuit.

MONOGRAMS & LETTERFORMS

A Monogram is a symbol designed using a combination of two or more letters, such as the logos for Hewlett-Packard and Warner Brothers.

A Letterform is similar but uses a single letter, such as the logos of McDonald's and Adobe.

Like symbols, Monograms and Letterforms may include a supporting wordmark. Alternatively, they can also be used on their own too.

ADVANTAGES

- It's quick and easy to explore ideas. Monograms and Letterforms are based on simple shapes, so you can often find interesting solutions that reference the business offering too.

- Compared with a wordmark, a Monogram or Lettermark will work more effectively at smaller sizes.

- If there's a supporting wordmark, you can create multiple lockups for greater versatility.

DISADVANTAGES

- A Monogram isn't always ideal if the company is an international organisation that requires a multilingual identity. In this case, a pictorial or abstract symbol that can be recognised globally may be more effective.

- When dealing with single letters, creating an original mark that's never been done before can be challenging.

WORDMARKS & LETTERMARKS

A Wordmark is a typography-based logo focusing only on the business name in a distinct font. Examples include Google and Disney.

Google **Disney**

A Lettermark is similar but features an abbreviation of the company's full name, such as BBC and NASA.

BBC NASA

Sometimes, a Lettermark could be mistaken for a monogram, but there are differences. Although a Lettermark also uses an abbreviation of the company name, it's how the business is known and referred to. This means that, unlike a monogram, it doesn't require a supporting wordmark. NASA is the perfect example. I doubt anyone refers to the company as "The National Aeronautics and Space Administration."

ADVANTAGES

- You instantly know the company name.

- Wordmarks and Lettermarks are often quicker and easier to design, especially when using an existing font.

DISADVANTAGES:

- They're not ideal for long names.

- They're often not distinct enough to be memorable.

It's common for a business to request a Lettermark logo, but I dislike abbreviations because it feels as though the name has lost its meaning.

Abbreviations can often have other meanings too. For instance, I recently passed by a company with the abbreviation STD, and it left me in fits of laughter.

Unless customers are already familiar with the abbreviated version of the name, I always advise the company to avoid this kind of logo. I usually recommend using the complete company name with a supporting symbol, shortening the existing name, or considering a new name. Ultimately, it's the owners' decision.

COMBINATION MARKS

A Combination Mark combines both a symbol and a wordmark.

Often, one or more of the letters has been designed to give a distinct look, or they're embedded within some kind of graphic element. Examples include Burger King and Walkers Crisps, also known as Lay's Potato Chips if you're not a Brit like me.

ADVANTAGES

- They can be distinct and memorable.

- You instantly know the company name.

- In cases where letters haven't been styled, they cross the language barrier, allowing the same consistent identity to be used globally.

DISADVANTAGES

- As the symbol and the typography are mixed together, in most cases, there can only be a single configuration of the logo, meaning that Combination Marks are less versatile.

EMBLEMS, CRESTS & BADGES

Emblems, Crests and Badges are similar to combination marks in how they combine image and text. The key difference is that the features are contained within a frame or border.

They're typically used by organisations with long-standing traditions or heritage, such as universities, sports teams, and government agencies. You often see them worn as badges and sewn onto clothing.

Examples include Harley Davidson, NFL, Harvard University and Mini.

ADVANTAGES

- Their classic appearance can be used to your advantage to convey a sense of unity, prestige or history.

- They're usually reasonably detailed, so they can include several intricate elements to tell a story or communicate different messages.

DISADVANTAGES

- They have limited versatility. They're often detailed, making them difficult to reproduce in small sizes and usually only have one configuration.

- Designing them can be challenging because they often include intricate details and patterns.

- They tend to follow a particular design style, making it harder to stand out in a crowded market where many Emblem logos are already in use.

MASCOTS

A logo that incorporates a Mascot can be categorised as a symbol or combination mark, although Mascots deserve recognition as a distinct category due to their unique impact.

Mascots come in a diverse range of forms, including people, animals, aliens, monsters, and even objects. While commonly associated with sports, schools, and children's cereals, their versatility extends across various industries. Notably, even insurance companies use mascots as part of their branding.

Mascots are not commonly integrated into logos, yet there are notable exceptions where they play a prominent role. For instance, consider the Michelin Man and the MailChimp Monkey as prime examples.

ADVANTAGES

- They can give a brand a lot of character and personality.

- They help to build a stronger relationship with customers.

- They can easily branch out from the logo to become a valuable asset for all kinds of marketing.

DISADVANTAGES

- They can be time-consuming to create.

- Cross-culturally, the Mascot may be engaging to some but offensive to others.

Now you know the types of logos available, let's dive into how to design them.

PART 2

DESIGN PROCESS

DESIGN ISN'T ALWAYS A LINEAR PROCESS, HOWEVER, YOU'LL OFTEN FOLLOW A SET OF STEPS FROM START TO FINISH.

IN THIS SECTION, I'LL SHARE A HIGH-LEVEL OVERVIEW OF MY DESIGN PROCESS.

SELL A PROCESS, NOT A LOGO

When businesses need a logo, they may invest anything from a few dollars up into the millions.

To the average person, the vast price difference is difficult to comprehend. But companies don't simply buy a logo… **they buy the expertise to create one and the process that goes along with it.**

This means that while two designers may offer a similar-looking end product at different price points, the process can differ drastically between one designer or agency and another.

At the lowest price point, the logo will be designed quickly… no research… no questions asked, and very little communication.

At the top end, a team of people will be involved over a longer period – not just designers but strategists, researchers, testers and more.

I price and position my services to attract companies that have been in business for several years, started on a bootstrap budget and can now invest in their identity. This also attracts startups that don't want to cut corners from the outset.

To accommodate this market, I've created what I feel is an effective process that can be completed in around 16–24 hours. This allows me to comfortably take on three to six projects per month, bringing in a healthy annual salary.

You don't need to do the same. You might prefer to take on fewer projects each month at a higher value, offering a more elaborate process. Or you can price your services low and do more projects in less time. There's a market for everyone, so the choice is yours.

Whatever method you choose, I recommend designing a process that you can work through repeatedly. This will be what you sell to clients, while also making your workflow easier and more predictable.

Let's dive into the design process I follow, which you're welcome to use as a starting point.

MY DESIGN PROCESS

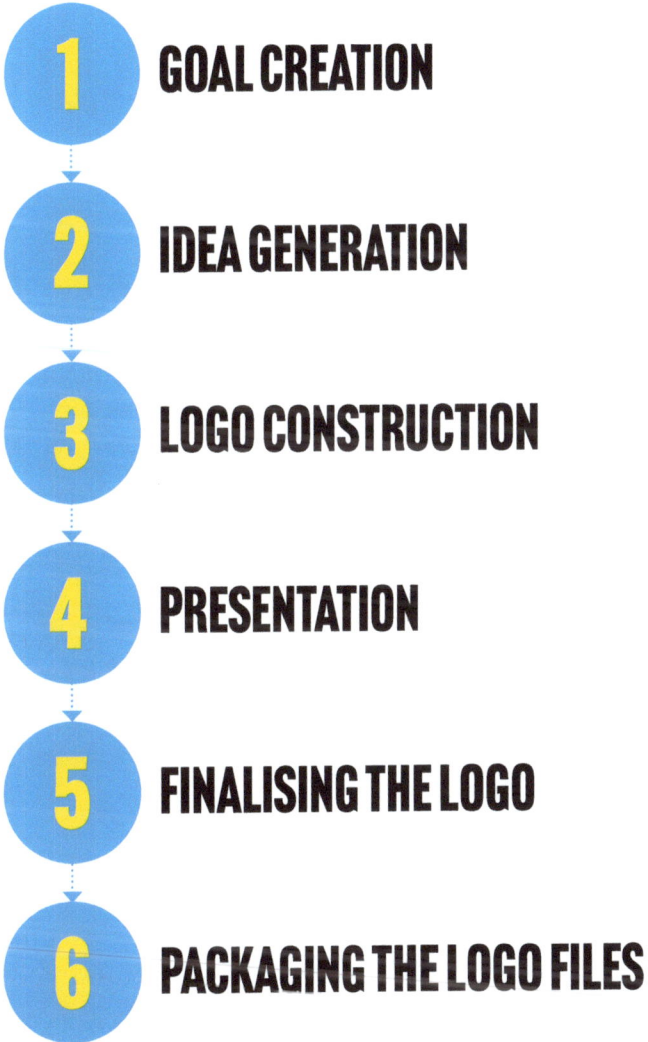

1 GOAL CREATION

2 IDEA GENERATION

3 LOGO CONSTRUCTION

4 PRESENTATION

5 FINALISING THE LOGO

6 PACKAGING THE LOGO FILES

STEP 1: GOAL CREATION

Before I can design a logo, I need to understand the business, its competition and its audience. I do this by sending my client a research and data-gathering questionnaire. Based on the responses, I create a list of goals that will aid my decisions during the design phase.

To learn how I create project goals, head to part three on page 40.

STEP 2: IDEA GENERATION

Using the goals as a target to aim at, I will use numerous idea-generation exercises that will allow me to sketch and explore a wide range of possible directions. I then select the best ideas to develop further.

To discover my techniques for idea generation, head to part four on page 50.

STEP 3: LOGO CONSTRUCTION

Using a computer and vector-based illustration software, I develop my chosen ideas further.

To learn how to construct a logo using professional design software, head to part five on page 74.

STEP 4: PRESENTATION

With a selection of designs ready, I prepare a presentation where I share each option individually, along with a series of images that show the logos in use on relevant items such as business cards, a shop exterior, clothing and more to help my client visualise the logo in real-life use. I then record a video, talking through the ideas while referencing back to the project goals.

To find out how I present logos to my clients, head to part six on page 116.

STEP 5: FINALISING THE LOGO

Once a design has been agreed upon, I refine and perfect the logo to ensure it's as perfect as possible.

To learn how I do this, head to part seven on page 134.

STEP 6: PACKAGING THE LOGO FILES

When the logo is complete and signed off by the client, I prepare a comprehensive logo package containing files for web and print use, along with a document to help my client understand how to use the different file formats. When payment is made, I transfer the files to my client.

To find out what files I prepare and how I send them, head to part eight on page 152.

PART 3

GOAL CREATION

TO UNDERSTAND WHAT YOU'RE TRYING TO ACHIEVE, YOU'LL NEED A PROJECT BRIEF.

IN THIS SECTION, I SHARE MY APPROACH FOR CREATING A BRIEF USING CLEARLY DEFINED PROJECT GOALS.

A TARGET TO AIM AT

It's easy to come up with ideas, however, to find the perfect solution, you'll need a target to aim at. In the design world, this target is known as a "design brief," a set of instructions that outline the desired results of a project.

There's no set way of writing a brief, but they'll always share the same purpose… to set out a list of goals and objectives. This is so that you understand what you're designing and why, and so both you and your client understand what the final outcome is intended to achieve.

Some clients may provide a brief, but most won't, so at the start of any project, I take the lead on its creation. I describe this as project goals, but its purpose is the same.

I work with my client to create a list of goals that covers three key areas of their company: their business, competition, and audience.

I ensure that the goals remain a consistent reference point throughout the project. Due to this, before moving forward with the design phase, I get approval in writing from my client, any decision-makers, and any other individuals who may provide feedback.

Logo design can easily be seen as art, so people will have subjective opinions when they first see a logo. However, when you design with strategic goals, you can explain decisions and refer back to the goals throughout the process.

Goals will encourage your clients to look at the designs objectively. It also establishes trust. You're more likely to get buy-in from the client and you will remain in control of the design phase.

To create the goals, I start by asking my client to complete a questionnaire. If required, I will follow up with additional questions to get any extra information I need.

Some designers dislike questionnaires, which I understand. When you have face-to-face discussions, you get to hear their stories and have the opportunity to dig deeper into their responses. My business started as a side venture, so the only time I had for such meetings was in my evenings - and that just wasn't practical. So a questionnaire had to make do.

Now I'm full-time, if the project requires it, I conduct a face-to-face interview, however, I still like to send a questionnaire for the bulk of my projects. I like that it gives clients time to think, research, and have necessary discussions. More importantly, it saves me time... and by saving time, I can offer a more cost-effective solution.

Remember that in-person (or virtual) discovery workshops can take up a lot of your valuable time. A discovery session can take several hours, sometimes even days, and you will probably provide valuable strategic insights and advice. So if it's something you choose to offer, make sure to factor that into the price, as it's a much more valuable service.

The questions I ask are broken down into three categories; The Business, The Competition and The Audience. I also like to gain an understanding of personal preferences and expectations too.

THE BUSINESS

- What is the name of your company?

- Do you have a company tagline or slogan?

- What product(s) or service(s) does your business provide?

- If you are not a new business startup, why do you want a new logo?

- Is there a unique story behind your business?

- Where do you see your business/service in five years?

- Where will your new logo be used?

THE COMPETITION

- Who are your main competitors?

- What differentiates you from your competitors?

- Why should your audience choose you over the competition?

THE AUDIENCE

- Who is your target audience?

- Describe your ideal customer.

- What is the overall message you want to convey to your target audience?

- What words do you want your audience to associate with your company?

PERSONAL PREFERENCE

The previous questions provide key strategic information about the business, however, I also like to ask questions to understand my client's preferences and expectations.

While personal preference is irrelevant to the solution, it's helpful to know this information because the client is paying for my time and will be the person giving feedback on the designs.

This ensures I have a clear idea of what they expect to see and can avoid presenting something I know they'll reject outright. It also gives me the opportunity to highlight and discuss any unusual suggestions that don't align with the companies goals.

Questions to understand preference include:

- What brands or logos, regardless of industry, capture a similar look and feel to what you are going for?

- Are there any fonts, colours, images or icons you want to see used in the logo?

- Are there any that you would like to see avoided?

Altogether, the questions help to give a solid understanding of the business and the client's expectations, however, if I feel I need further information or have questions that expand on anything that's been said, I will speak with my client to fill in the gaps.

Using the collated information, I summarise the responses into a bullet-pointed list of goals that will act as a tick-list that I can follow while I work on the designs. I also refer back to it when presenting the designs.

On the following pages is an example I put together before designing the logo for the **International Centre for Eye Health (ICEH)**, who undertake research and education to improve eye health worldwide. To donate to their work, visit: **iceh.lshtm.ac.uk/donate**

LOGO DESIGN GOALS FOR INTERNATIONAL CENTRE FOR EYE HEALTH (ICEH)

- To design a logo for International Centre for Eye Health (ICEH).

- For reference, the company slogan is "Improving Eye Health Worldwide."

- To represent an organisation that:

  > Is part of the London School of Hygiene and Tropical Medicine (LSHTM), but are semi-independent.

  > Is working to improve eye health worldwide.

  > Is improving eye health in lower and middle-income countries, including Africa and some areas of South and South-East Asia.

  > Carries out research projects, training, education and technology. For example, Tanzania does not have enough ophthalmologists to cover the population, so a large research project was carried out to train nurses to use a new low-cost tool that would detect childhood eye health problems.

  > Ensure that people in lower-income countries access the same treatments available in higher-income countries.

  > Has an international team with alumni from over 100 countries worldwide.

> Frequently works in partnership with other people, such as the World Health Organisation (WHO) and other prominent international bodies.

> Publish *The Community Eye Health Journal.* This free print journal shares articles with eye health workers in Africa and India to help improve their work.

- A redesign is required as the current/old logo is considered to be "clunky" and doesn't work effectively in all instances.

- The logo must be sufficiently versatile to work effectively on a website, social media and printed marketing material.

- There are no direct competitors. However, some of the main partners include:

  > sightsavers.org

  > iapb.org

  > hollows.org

  > rcophth.ac.uk

- To appeal to organisations and personnel such as the WHO, eye care professionals and doctors.

- The ideal target customer is an ophthalmologist in Tanzania who wants to help improve eye care in their country, or is an advocacy specialist at an international non-profit organisation.

- The logo should aim to communicate that ICEH is the go-to source for eye health information and can provide support to improve eye health worldwide.

- Where possible, the logo should aim to relate to the following words: International, Equality, Democratic, Accessible, Research and Benefit.

- Organisations that capture the desired look and feel include:

  > ARVO (The Association for Research in Vision and Ophthalmology)

  > Moorfields Eye Hospital

- Reference the LSHTM guidelines when choosing a colour palette which many of the university centres align with, however, open to advice if an alternative route is recommended.

- As the target audience may have visual impairments, the logo should use clear and accessible fonts for people with reduced vision. Open to suggestions; however, the website uses the font Roboto and Open Sans, and the LSHTM guidelines use Messina and Merriweather.

- Avoid using yellow, as Sightsavers, one of the company's partners, use it heavily.

- Avoid anything too close to the "all-seeing eye" due to long-held superstitions in Africa.

- Preferably, the new logo should be circular so that it can be easily used independently from the centre name, which is a constraint of the current logo.

The Old Logo

If you would like to see the idea generation sketches for ICEH, head to pages 54 and 55, and to see the final solution, head to pages 63 and 136.

GETTING THE GOALS APPROVED

Once the goals are created, I get my point of contact, the decision-maker, and anyone else who might be involved in the process, to check and approve them in writing before I proceed with any designs. This ensures that everyone involved in the project is working towards the same goal. It also sets the expectation that decisions will be strategic, and helps to ensure that feedback during the presentation remains as objective as possible.

This approach also keeps me in control. Consider a scenario where, after approval, the client wants to alter the goals, despite a significant investment of time in the creative process. In this example, I have solid grounds to request additional costs to cover my time. It also discourages any third party, with a different vision, from offering unsolicited opinions, as the project's direction has already been agreed upon.

Now that we have goals prepared, let's dive into how to prepare logo ideas.

PART 4

IDEA GENERA-TION

USUALLY, THE MOST CHALLENGING, TIME-CONSUMING PART OF LOGO DESIGN IS COMING UP WITH A GOOD IDEA.

IN THIS SECTION, I'LL SHARE THE TECHNIQUES I USE TO TRANSLATE GOALS INTO HUNDREDS OF IDEAS & HOW TO SELECT THE BEST OF THEM TO DEVELOP FURTHER.

A JOURNEY OF DISCOVERY

Once the goals are signed off, I'm ready to proceed to the design phase. This is where I translate all the gathered information into an effective logo design.

To help you understand how I work, in this section I'll share the idea-generation exercises I use. This might sound like I follow a linear process, although that's never the case.

Once I open my sketchbook, I let the ideas flow, hopping back and forth between the exercises. Sometimes I get lucky and have a strong idea right away, other times I struggle. Regardless, I trust the process and keep persevering until I've found the perfect solution.

I like to print off the goals and read through them carefully several times. I then highlight any words or phrases that could influence the design, however, before sketching ideas, there's a few things I like to do…

STUDY THE COMPETITIVE LANDSCAPE

To understand the competitive landscape, I visit the websites of all the competitors mentioned and any others I found when performing my research. I then copy and paste the logos into a Photoshop document for reference. This allows me to make informed decisions to ensure the logo I design differentiates my client's brand from the competition.

PINPOINT THE DESIRED AESTHETIC

When I started designing logos, I focused on developing clever ideas. The more clever they were, the better. However, after several years of study, I realised my approach needed to be corrected. Instead, you need to discover the solution with the right "feel and aesthetic" for the business.

Early in my career, I was lucky enough to spend time with logo and font specialist, Miles Newlyn, who designed logos for companies including Sky, EE and Unilever. He introduced me to a valuable thought exercise I will share with you.

Imagine the company you're designing the logo for dropped a leaflet through your door. What would you expect to pick up? What does it look like? How does it feel? What's the weight of the paper and finish? Is it high-end, minimal and luxurious? Is it formal and professional? Is it fun and playful? Or does it feel like a budget, low-cost service?

What you picture will be drawn from your personal experiences. Where you work, where you've travelled to, the places you shop, the films and TV programmes you watch, what you read and where you eat will all contribute to a mental toolbox of aesthetics and visual associations that you can draw from, so be sure to experience all the wonders of life.

In doing this exercise, a picture of the leaflet might come into my mind in seconds, but from time-to-time, I need to create a mood board to give myself more clarity.

I compile things with the appropriate aesthetic, including images, fonts, colours, paper samples and more. I look in books and magazines and on Google, Pinterest, Behance and Dribbble.

I'm not searching for ideas, but instead focusing on what I believe has the appropriate aesthetic and what 'feels' right. I then paste everything into a large Photoshop document for reference. Knowing the overall aesthetic I want provides clarity, making idea generation more focused too.

I don't share my mood boards with my clients, but I know plenty of designers who do. Some even create several, each focusing on different aspects of the goals. These are used to discuss ideas and agree on a direction. This is particularly useful if you're designing the entire supporting identity, as you can explore the possibilities without investing too much time.

SKETCHING IDEAS

At this point, I jump into my sketchbook. It doesn't matter what type of paper and pencil you use, but I like to use an A4 hardback dotted notebook from Leuchtturm1917, along with a retractable pencil.

In the past, as I had a large desk, I used A1 sheets of paper that filled my desk. Now I prefer the practicality of an A4 book. It's easier to store and archive, and allows me to sketch at my desk or anywhere else I feel comfortable to do so, such as on the sofa, in a café or even on a park bench.

Sketches/ideas for the International Centre for Eye Health logo, by Ian Paget

23.4°

Whatever you do, I recommend not simply diving onto your computer without a prepared direction. As you're working with perfect shapes, an idea can look finished too early and will lack personality.

Sketching, in comparison, is faster and a little unpredictable, meaning that happy accidents can happen. I've often scribbled an idea so imperfectly that it's sparked a whole new concept I would never have considered any other way. Plus, I spend most of my day staring at a screen, so I love the escape and freedom that a sketchbook offers.

I know some designers who prefer to use tablet computers, which now have a near-identical feel to actual paper. This might be a preferred option for you too.

Without a good idea, you have no logo, so generating ideas is the most crucial step of the process. Staring at a blank piece of paper can be daunting, so I carry out a few idea-generation exercises to help me along the way. Let's dive into each of these.

That's me, sketching ideas.

WORD MAPPING

Word mapping is a fantastic technique to help me think of ideas outside the box.

I start by writing down a word related to the business in the middle of a piece of paper. The word can be connected to the company name, the type of products or services they offer, their tagline, their values… anything that could help me generate ideas. I then draw lines extending from this and add as many associated words as possible. To speed this up, I frequently use a thesaurus.

For example, suppose I was designing a logo for a property letting company. In that case, I might start with the words "estate agent." I would then add associated words around that, such as rent, house, moving, property, and flat. From the word "moving," I would add words like delivery van, boxes, packing, and tape. I'll then repeat the exercise for as many words as needed to spark ideas.

While writing down words, I frequently picture a potential idea, and I'll sketch that out before returning to my word map, where I'll keep adding words to ensure I explore all the possibilities.

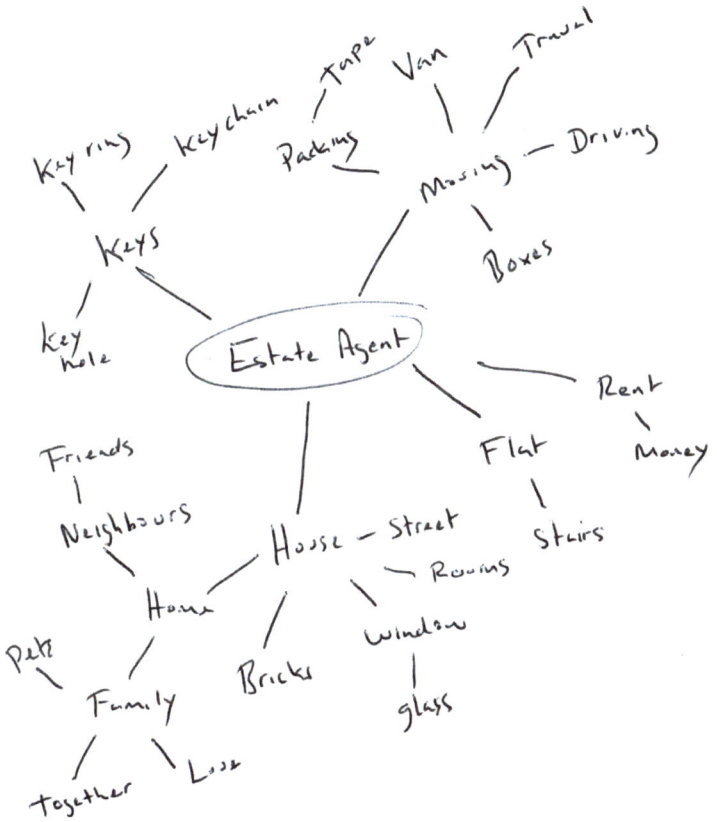

PICTURE MIX & MATCH

Another exercise that I like to do in combination with word mapping is to draw icons, shapes and symbols related to the words.

Search Engines, such as Google, can be a handy tool for this exercise. I search one of the words written down followed by "symbol," which will display pages of everyday objects, icons and marks associated with that word. I sketch everything I see, and look for opportunities to combine things to create a new symbol.

For example, I worked on the logo for Astro Blue Properties, an estate agent based in Manchester, UK. I first googled "estate agent symbols," where I came across images such as houses, keys, contracts and location pins. I then googled "space symbols," where I found rockets, planets, aliens, telescopes, moons and satellites.

It was only when everything was roughly sketched on paper that I noticed I could combine a rocket shape with a house, resulting in a really effective solution for the business. By a happy accident, the combined shapes also work well as an abstract "A" lettermark.

I used this same approach when designing the logo for the International Centre for Eye Health, whose project goals I shared earlier in the book (see pages 46-48).

To convey the organisation's mission of addressing vision loss and recovery, I combined an eye with a solar eclipse. This was achieved by creating a circular shape that was divided down the middle and tilted at a 23.5-degree angle, referencing the Earth's tilt. One side of the circle features light rays, while the other depicts the same, but

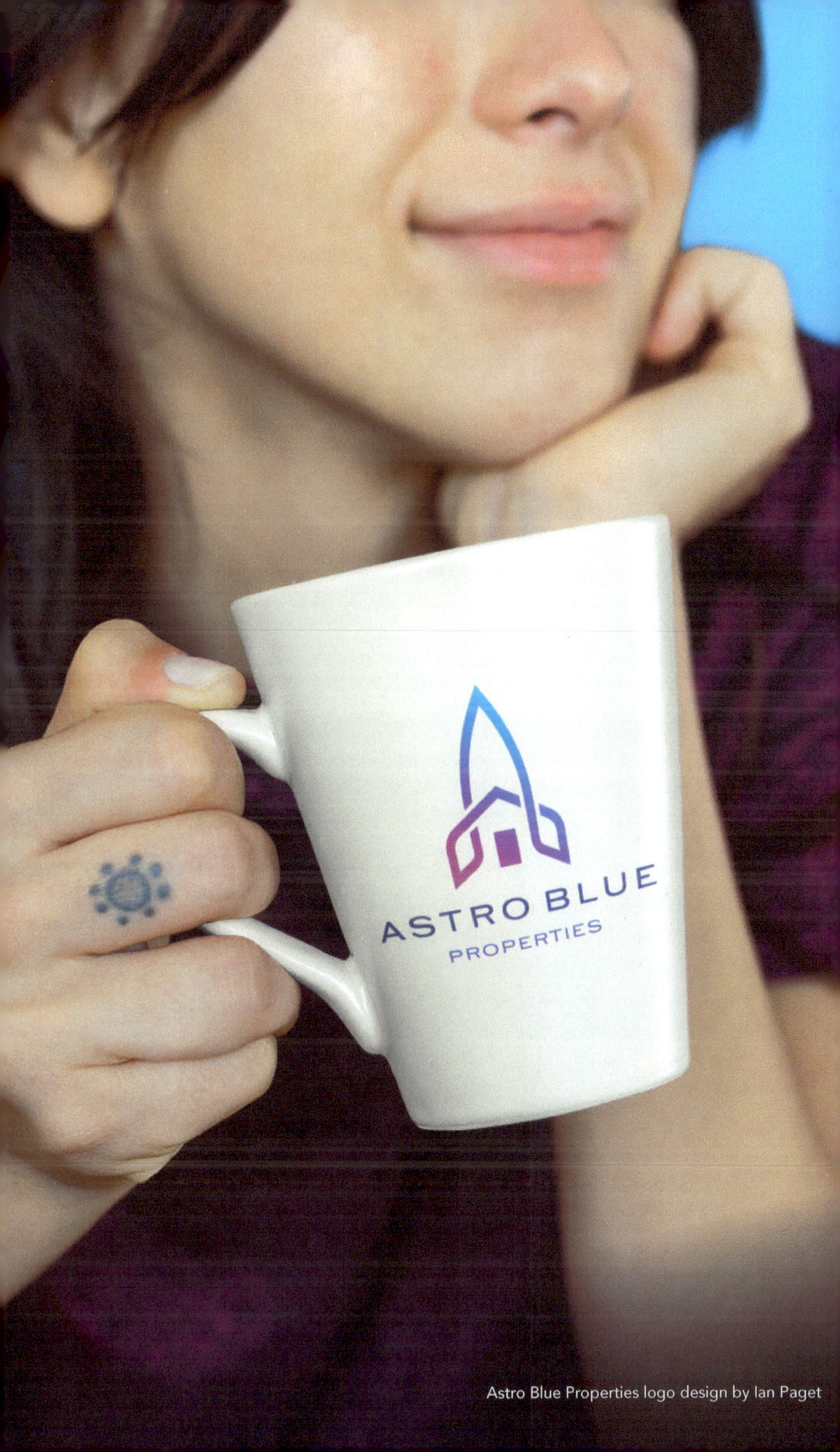

Astro Blue Properties logo design by Ian Paget

in the negative. This symbolic representation of light and darkness represents the centre's aim of promoting eye health and fighting against visual impairment.

CAN YOU TELL A STORY?

One of my favourite approaches to idea generation is to visually tell a story. You can draw this from the project goals, or any further reading you might do on the business or service offering. For example, I worked on a logo for a business called Soul Somatic Therapy, which offers a type of treatment called Somatic Experiencing (SE), designed to help heal trauma and other stress-related disorders.

This therapy works on sensations in the body that may become trapped after a stressful experience. The concept is that by directing attention towards these sensations, like the emotion of anger, our body can naturally respond to the previously suppressed instinct for action. Carrying out this action helps resolve the previously stagnant impulses, addressing the root cause of trauma symptoms.

Through research, I discovered that ancient indigenous communities, like those from the Amazon rainforest, have healing systems that draw on the body's natural healing energy in the same way as "SE." For reference, I looked into tribal ceramics, body paint, headdresses and art, and I discovered swirl-like symbols, representing energy, were used throughout.

The final logo includes two of these "energy" swirls that form the letter "S," which also helps to visually explain "SE." The first swirl represents the original trauma. The second then shows the trauma being experienced a second time in the form of therapy. To display the release of pain, lines shine out from the second swirl like sun rays.

International Centre for Eye Health logo design by Ian Paget

THE FOUR CATEGORIES

In Michael Shumate's book, "*Logo Design Theory*," he theorised that logo concepts are broken down into only four categories. These are: Corporate Activity, Corporate Ideals, Corporate Name and Abstract. This can provide a framework to reference when generating ideas.

Corporate Activity describes the logos that show something about the product or the company's activity. For example, the World Wildlife Fund (WWF) shows a giant panda to symbolise endangered species, the US Open Tennis Championships uses a tennis ball in flight, and a burger is used in the Burger King logo.

Corporate Ideals reference qualities or ideals the company aspires to, such as superiority, strength, speed or accuracy. This can be seen in the Nike swoosh, designed to represent a wing of the Greek goddess of victory. The Barclays' logo features the heraldic eagle, representing courage and power, and the Premier League logo features a lion, which is depicted in English heraldry, implying belonging to royal blood.

Corporate Name is a logo that simply references the name of the company. This often has nothing to do with the product or service itself. For example, the apple in the Apple logo, the bell in the Taco Bell logo, and the whirl in the Whirlpool logo.

Abstract logos say very little about the company but can be unique and distinct. For example, the Slack logo includes a stylised hashtag, the Mitsubishi logo has its three-diamond symbol, and the McDonald's logo features its golden arches.

If you consider that you only have three possible components to work with – a wordmark, lettermark or symbol – then you can easily plan out potential ideas for each, considering these four concepts. If you were to sketch just one idea for each, you'd immediately have twelve ideas... and if you sketched out three for each, you'd quickly have thirty-six!

DESIGN THE NEGATIVE SPACE

When you're designing on a white background, your eyes will focus on everything in colour. However, when you invert the design and place it onto black, the negative space will become much more visible than expected. That means that if there are any unusual shapes, they might become an unwanted distraction, so be sure to consciously design the negative space in your logo.

Occasionally, you can take advantage of it, making the negative space a design feature. For example, when working on the logo for Conservation Evidence, a resource to support those making decisions about maintaining and restoring biodiversity, I developed an idea that combined a book with the leaves of a sprouting plant.

By a happy accident, I noticed that the negative space could resemble a tree of life, so I further developed the logo so that the tree became a prominent feature of the design.

Conservation Evidence logo design by Ian Paget

USE SEMIOTICS

One question you might have when translating the project goals is how do you know what style is right? What font? What shapes? I could give surface-level advice, but if you understand semiotics, you can start to answer these questions independently.

From the moment we're born into this world, we begin to learn from our experiences – what we hear, see, touch, and smell. We start associating colours, shapes, and forms with different aspects of life. For instance, when we see traffic lights, we collectively understand that red signifies stop, while green means go. If I were to ask you to assign colours to boys and girls, I can safely assume that most people would choose blue for boys and pink for girls.

This isn't knowledge we're born with; rather, it is taught and has evolved over time within the cultural we live in. We carry cultural lessons like this with us through life, so when we encounter a brand for the first time, we'll use all our cultural experiences to help figure out what the brand is about. That's what semiotics is. It's the study of signs and symbols (words, images, sounds, gestures and objects) and tries to unpack how meaning is created.

I interviewed consumer psychologist Dr. Rachel Lawes (listen @ logogeek.uk/81), who wrote the book "*Using Semiotics in Marketing.*" Rachel is fascinated by the semiotics of weddings and explained in our interview that in the Western world, brides aspire for their weddings to be different, special, and unique to them. However, what makes any event special are its repetitive features. In the case of weddings, it's the dress, bridesmaids, ceremony, etc. If too many of these features were taken away, it would no longer feel like a wedding. This is because all the semiotic signs that define it as a wedding would be stripped away.

This logic also applies to logo design, which is why I mentioned the importance of appropriateness earlier. While differentiation is vital, if you're designing an identity for an accounting business, you'll want to tap into all of the cultural cues that make it feel trustworthy and credible. This will naturally determine font styles and colours. If you don't leverage these attributes, you'll face an uphill battle to re-educate the masses.

The world is full of visual cues that we can use to subconsciously communicate a message and add meaning to a logo design.

If you're anything like me, understanding the role of semiotics will open your eyes. You'll start to learn from everything around you. You'll become more observant, will ask more questions, and will be open to new experiences that allow you to better understand the symbols you see in your environment and where their meaning has come from.

SKETCH EVERYTHING... EVEN BAD IDEAS

I see so many perfectly drawn-out logos when browsing social media, which can be intimidating for those new to the industry. Here, what you're seeing is the refined sketch and not the planning and development that went into it, which is usually messy scribbles. When you're generating ideas, only you need to see that. It doesn't matter what they look like. Scribble, play and have fun. Get the ideas out of your head... even the rubbish ideas.

It's normal to think up boring, unoriginal, or silly ideas, which most might immediately dismiss. However, I draw them anyway. Once they're on paper, I often realise they have potential, or they may form the foundation of an unexpected idea that I wouldn't have considered if I didn't sketch the bad ideas.

Let ideas develop on paper rather than in your head. Don't sit thinking about them. Just draw and keep drawing.

I usually sketch hundreds of ideas – sometimes the same idea repeatedly with slight variations, however, I'll keep going until I have a handful of solid ideas that I feel have real potential to develop. I never stop at just one good idea. I keep experimenting to explore the full potential of the project.

I like to spend at least a day, if not more, exploring ideas on paper, as having a good idea is the most crucial part of the design process. It's also substantially faster to explore on paper, so I'll keep going until I have a solid plan before jumping into Adobe Illustrator.

COMBATING CREATIVE BLOCK

Hopefully, the techniques described in this section will help you explore many great ideas. Unless you're insanely gifted, coming up with an original logo that correctly represents the business and differentiates it from the competition is really hard.

Because it's hard, you'll frequently feel that you're making no progress or that you've hit what's commonly referred to as a "creative block." But don't worry! It happens to everyone.

That's me (or rather my hand), sketching, using a retractable pencil

I've had days when I've worked all day long sketching ideas, only to reach the end of the day without a single good idea. That feeling sucks, but I keep going and accept that the muddy mess of exploring ideas is part of the design process. I often have hundreds of terrible scribbles and weak ideas, but I only need one incredible idea, so I keep going until I find it.

When I feel utterly drained of ideas, I take a break. I go for a walk. I get some rest. I play a game. I do the washing up. I will sleep on it if needed. I almost always return with a fresh perspective and often find that during the time away, without even thinking about the project, I dream up unexpected ideas. Ideas can come from weird places, so don't give up! Trust the process.

SELECT THE BEST IDEAS

Once I have several pages of scribbles, notes, and ideas and feel that I've exhausted the possibilities, I'll pick up my highlighter pen and circle the ideas I think are the strongest. My ultimate goal is to find the most suitable logo for the business, so I'll always refer back to the project's goals when choosing.

Most of my ideas will be awful, although a few always have real potential. Usually, one or two are very strong and fill me with excitement, so I always circle those. There might be one or two directions that have something happening and need further development, so I circle them too.

Most of the time, after selecting a few directions, even if they're rough, I proceed to develop them on a computer, which I discuss in the next part of this book.

Occasionally, when a design proves to be particularly intricate or I need a break from the computer screen, I do most of my development and exploration on paper. In such instances, tracing paper proves to be an invaluable tool, which was frequently used by logo designers before computers came along.

The process involves sketching out a concept on paper, then overlaying tracing paper on top to refine and explore the possibilities of the design. You can layer as many sheets of tracing paper as necessary, enabling you to refine and revise the design as many times as you wish until you feel that you have achieved perfection.

PART 5

LOGO CONSTRUC-TION

NOW IT'S TIME TO TURN THOSE SKETCHES INTO PROFESSIONAL VECTOR ARTWORK.

IN THIS SECTION, YOU'LL FIND OUT HOW I CREATE WELL-EXECUTED ARTWORK, THE OPTICAL ILLUSIONS I CONSIDER, & HOW I CHOOSE FONTS & COLOURS.

SKETCH TO VECTOR

Once you have several solid ideas, you will need a computer and the appropriate software to prepare professional artwork.

The exact type of computer you will use will depend on your budget and preferences; luckily, the software needed to design logos is not processor-heavy, so the average computer will do the job. Just double-check the system requirements of your chosen software to be sure.

At the time of writing, I use a Mac Pro with a separate 32-inch monitor. It's an expensive setup, but I use it daily for client work, so having the speed and power has been worth the investment. I've been an Apple fanboy for a long time, so I prefer to use a Mac, which I'm used to. A Windows PC is perfectly sufficient for logo design too.

The downside with Apple is that you pay a premium. To make it more affordable, I purchase second-hand through sites like eBay or Facebook Marketplace. Many photographers and studios want the latest and greatest equipment, so they'll upgrade and sell their kit after only a year or two. Buying it from them means I get a much higher specification computer for my money. If you spend time looking, they're usually well looked after and in their original packaging too, and since Apple hardware retains its value, I keep the box and sell it on a few years later to contribute to my next upgrade.

With the hardware in place, now we need software. There are two types of image editors: raster and vector.

A raster graphics editor like Adobe Photoshop is excellent for compositing images. While it's possible to design logos in it, when you begin to scale the image, you'll notice that it's composed of small squares called pixels, which makes it an unsuitable format for logo design. Instead, you should consider using a vector graphics editor.

Vector graphics are based on paths, points, lines, curves, and shapes using mathematical equations instead of pixels. This means they can be scaled indefinitely without any loss of quality. The vector editor I use is Adobe Illustrator, which has remained the industry standard for many years.

The monthly subscription puts some people off Adobe. However, if you're designing logos for a living, it's a worthwhile investment. It's feature-rich, with powerful tools that allow you to quickly build and edit any shape you can imagine, and there's also a wide range of plug-ins that extend its capabilities. For example, I use LiveSurface, Astute Graphics, and Logo Package Express, which I discuss later in this book.

If you prefer a one-off cost, I recommend Affinity Designer, part of the "Affinity Trinity" alongside Affinity Photo and Affinity Publisher. If you want something that costs you nothing, the closest free alternatives to Adobe Illustrator I've seen are Inkscape and Vectornator, which both have similar drawing tools.

Once you have a computer and software, you can now turn your ideas into professional-looking logos, which I discuss next. Since I use Adobe Illustrator, the steps discussed in this book will be geared toward an Adobe user; however, the techniques should still apply to other software.

Here, I'm using Adobe Illustrator on an iMac, which I used for years before upgrading to a more powerful Mac Pro.

A BRIEF OVERVIEW OF ADOBE ILLUSTRATOR

As software constantly evolves, I won't dive too deep into the tools in this book since the information will soon become obsolete. Instead, I recommend you check out up-to-date tutorials to learn the software's full capabilities. You'll find some suggestions at the back of this book (page 290).

That said, I believe several core features will remain relevant for some time, so by sharing them here, I hope you'll be able to quickly get up to speed and start constructing your logo ideas right away!

The interface can look daunting at first, but to help you get started, let's focus on 4 key areas: the **Menu Bar** at the top, the **Artboard** in the middle, the **Toolbar** on the left, and the **Properties Panel** on the right.

MENU BAR

The menu bar runs across the top of the screen, where you'll see headings such as File, Edit, Object, and Type. Using these dropdowns, you can perform actions such as creating a new document and saving it. You can do more than this, but that's all we'll focus on now.

The Menu Bar

The Artboard

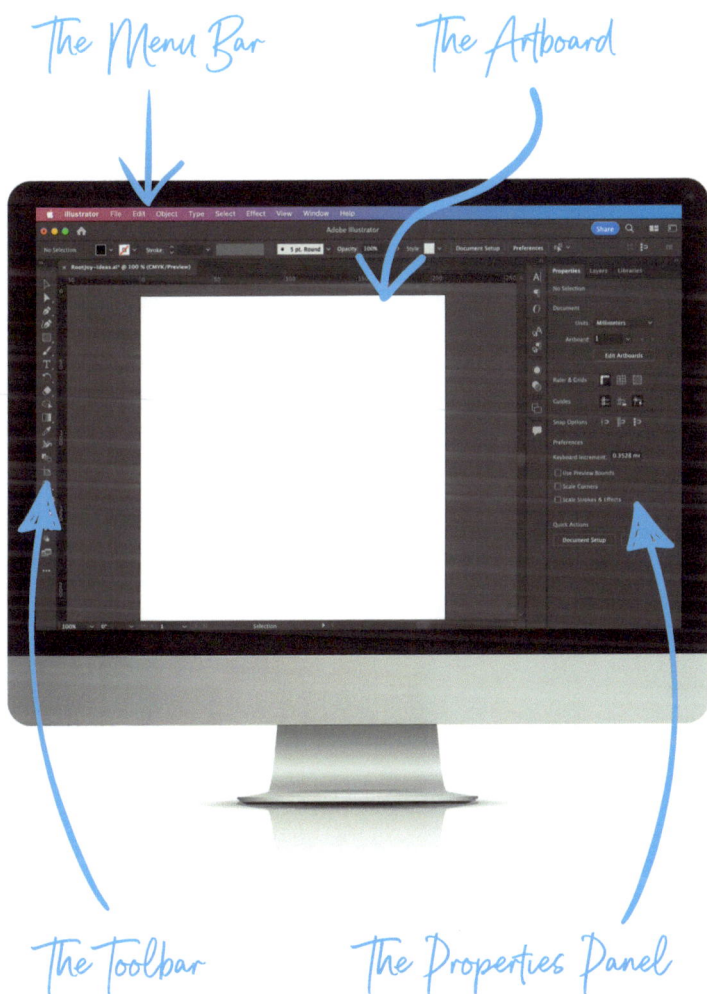

The Toolbar

The Properties Panel

ARTBOARD

The white box in the middle of the screen is the artboard. You can think of this as a piece of paper and the surrounding area as a desk.

Anything you create on the artboard will be visible when you save the file as a PDF or place it into another software such as InDesign. The surrounding area will be invisible, so you can use this area to drop anything you just want to keep for reference.

When working on ideas, it doesn't matter what size it is, but I start with A4. Only once the design is complete will I size the artboard to fit the design.

It's also possible to add multiple artboards, which can be helpful if you want to design a multiple-page document, but when designing logos, you only need one.

TOOLBAR

The toolbar panel on the left is where you'll find the tools.

Here's a breakdown of those you'll use most frequently when designing a logo.

THE PEN TOOL

The Pen tool allows you to create any shape you can imagine. To use it, select the tool, click anywhere on the artboard, then move the cursor to a different area and click again to create a line.

Now move your cursor to a different location and click again. Then return to the first point you added and click it to close the path. You should hopefully have drawn a triangle.

Now, I want you to move your cursor to a different place on the artboard. Click to start drawing a new shape, then move your cursor over and click again. This time I want you to keep your finger down and pull. You'll start to see a curve forming, and as you pull back, the curve gets more intense, and if you change the angle, the curve changes too. Once you're happy with the shape, let go and click at another location. You have now drawn what is known as a Bézier curve!

Play around with the tool to get a feel for drawing different shapes. Don't worry too much about getting the shape perfect the first time, as you'll be able to modify the shape with the Selection Tool, which we'll get into shortly.

A couple of extra things worth knowing: if you hold down the Shift key when drawing, it will lock to 45 degrees, and if you want to go from a Bézier curve to a square corner, hold down the Alt key and click the point.

The Pen tool will be one of the most essential tools you'll use in Illustrator, so learn to master it. To practice, you might find it helpful to play the Bézier Game to hone your skills, which you can find by heading to bezier.method.ac.

SELECTION TOOL & DIRECT SELECTION TOOL

At the top of the toolbar, you'll see two icons: a black arrow and a white arrow.

The black arrow is the Selection tool, which you use to select and move whole objects.

The white arrow is the Direct Selection tool, which allows you to select and modify individual points within an object. For example, if you've drawn a Bézier curve and it's not quite perfect, you can use this tool to refine it.

SHAPE TOOL

Aside from the Pen tool, logos are usually constructed using a combination of shapes. In Illustrator, you have access to a Rectangle tool, Ellipse tool, Polygon tool, and Star tool. These are grouped together on the toolbar. To access them, click and hold the shape icon to preview the available shapes.

To draw a shape, click on the artboard and drag until you reach the desired size. If you hold down Shift, the proportions will remain equal.

When using the Polygon or Star tool, if you press the up and down arrows on your keyboard while drawing your shape, you can add or subtract sides to it.

TYPE TOOL

The Type tool allows you to add text to your design. To use it, select the tool and click anywhere on the artboard. If you click once, you can type as you wish; if you click and drag, you will create a text box.

Within the Properties Panel on the right, you can control the type attributes, such as font, size, kerning, and tracking.

If you select and hold down the Type tool icon in the Tools menu, you'll have access to other associated features such as "type on path." To use this, first, draw a shape, such as a circle, then select the "type on path" tool and click on the shape created to add text that wraps around it.

REFLECT & ROTATE TOOLS

Like the Shape tool, the Reflect and Rotate tools are grouped under one button on the toolbar.

To use either of these tools, first, use the Selection tool to highlight the object you want to reflect or rotate. To reflect the object, select the Reflect tool, then hit the return key on your keyboard. You'll see a window where you're presented with different options. Choose your options, then hit OK.

To rotate the object, after highlighting it, select the Rotate tool, then click and drag up and down anywhere on the artboard.

SHAPE BUILDER TOOL

The Shape Builder tool combines objects to create new shapes.

To see the tool in action, draw several overlapping shapes on the artboard, then use the Selection tool to highlight them. Now select the Shape Builder tool from the toolbar and click and drag over two intersecting parts of the shape to combine them. If you hold down the Alt key and do the same, it will delete the shapes instead.

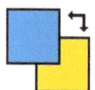

FILL & STROKE COLOUR

At the bottom of the toolbar, you'll notice two overlapping squares representing an object's fill and stroke colours.

Select the square furthest to the left to control the fill colour; select the square on the right to control the stroke colour. Clicking on the arrow swaps the fill and stroke colours, then double-clicking on either square, and you'll be presented with a colour picker, where you'll be able to choose a colour.

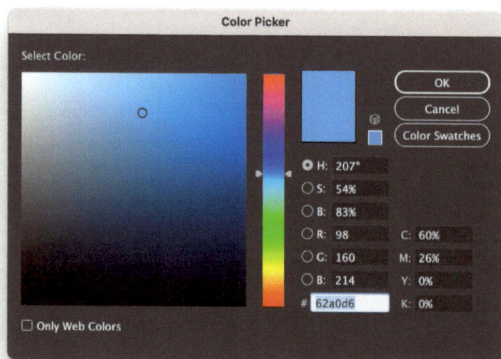

PROPERTIES PANEL

On the right-hand side of the interface, you'll see the Properties Panel.

If you select an object, in this panel, you can change the object's appearance, including stroke weight. If you've selected a piece of type, you can control the font, size, and other preferences.

The Properties Panel offers numerous other capabilities, but this should suffice for now.

PATHFINDER PANEL

When designing logos, you will need to combine multiple shapes. You can use either the Pathfinder Panel or the Shape Builder tool, which we have already discussed. Both combine objects to create new shapes but operate in slightly different ways.

The Pathfinder Panel can be accessed by going to the main menu, selecting Window, and then choosing Pathfinder from the dropdown.

Once you see the Pathfinder Panel, which you'll find to the right of the interface, you'll notice ten small icons. The icons in the top row are shape modes, which unite or exclude shapes to create a single object. The icons across the bottom row are known as pathfinders, which break up the shapes to create separate objects.

To try this out, draw and select one or more overlapping shapes, then choose one of the following buttons from the panel to perform the desired action.

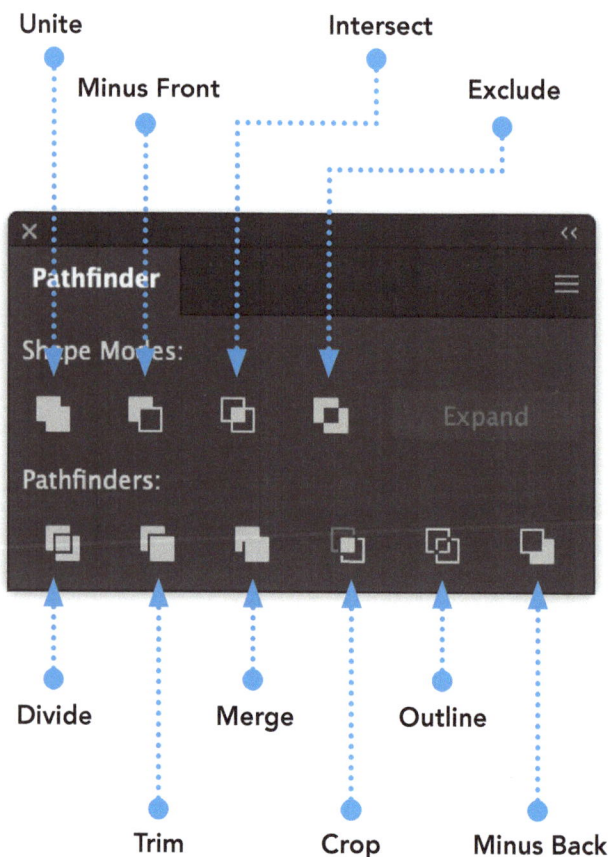

- **Unite** combines two or more shapes into one object.

- **Minus Front** removes the top shape from the shape below it.

- **Intersect** creates a shape based on the overlapping area.

- **Exclude** removes the overlapping area.

- **Divide** breaks up the overlapping shapes into separate objects.

- **Trim** cuts away the top shape from the shape below it.

- **Merge** is similar to Trim, however, in this case, it merges the objects with the same colour and trims the outline of the shape below it.

- **Crop** removes everything outside boundary of the object that sits on the top.

- **Outline** creates separate outlines of the shapes selected. These outlines can then be individually selected and ungrouped.

- **Minus Back** is the opposite of Minus Front, so it removes the bottom shape from the shape above it.

ZOOM & MOVE SHORTCUTS

When creating logos, you'll want to quickly and easily zoom in and out and move around the artboard effortlessly. Knowing the shortcuts for this will drastically speed up your workflow.

To zoom in and out, hold down the Command key on your keyboard, then press the Plus key to zoom in or the Minus key to zoom out.

To move around the artboard quickly, simply hold down the space bar while clicking and dragging anywhere on your artboard.

FURTHER LEARNING

There are many more tools and features in Adobe Illustrator beyond this, although I hope that knowing these basic features will help you to quickly start creating logos.

To get a feel for the other tools, I like to click and see what happens and slowly work my way around the software.

I do, however, encourage you to seek out tutorials or take a course to enhance your abilities. Head to the Further Learning & Support section (page 290) at the back of this book, where you'll find a list of training courses.

FONTS

A logo usually comprises two core elements: type and a symbol.

I see so many designers putting all their time and energy into creating a symbol, while the font choice is often an afterthought. This is understandable because a symbol is often the most distinct element and the most interesting to design. Plus, on top of this, almost all logo books and galleries focus on the symbol too.

Because the company's name is a fundamental part of the logo, I typically select a font first. This choice helps to establish the desired personality, character, and style of the logo as a whole.

WHERE TO FIND FONTS

There are thousands of fonts out there. Your computer will come with a few installed already. However, to create a distinct logo, you'll want to build your own font library.

Some fonts are free, but for most, you will need to pay for a license to use them. If you have an Adobe subscription, you'll have free access to Adobe Fonts, which is often the first place I look.

A great alternative is Google Fonts, which are free to use commercially. Because they're open source, you're able to customise them too.

You might come across other websites with free fonts, but use them cautiously. If you want to use a font for a logo, you must have a commercial license; however, most free fonts online are free for personal use only, meaning they cannot be used within a logo. There are, however, a few genuinely free commercial fonts out there. One website that's done the hard work for you is Font Squirrel, which has made it easy to search, view, and download free commercial fonts.

Design blogs also frequently collate the best free fonts from the web, so it's worth keeping an eye out and downloading them for future use. A quick Google search for "free commercial fonts" will lead you to many such posts.

The downside to free fonts is that they are often either poorly designed or overused, diluting any effort to create a distinct logo. For this reason, well-designed fonts are a worthwhile investment. To purchase fonts, MyFonts is a good place to start. I have listed several resources and font foundries at the back of this book to supplement your search (page 300).

CHOOSING A FONT

Selecting a font can sometimes feel overwhelming due to the multitude of options available. However, as various fonts have distinct attributes and personalities, I refer to the project goals to assist in selecting the most suitable style for the project.

For example, a serif typeface will be an ideal choice if I want a classic, traditional look. A slab serif font could work for something a little more vintage and masculine. A sans-serif font is ideal if I want a modern, simple, clean design. Script fonts can often feel feminine, ornate, and elegant. Handwritten fonts can work well if I want something a little more fun and playful.

Fonts are fascinating. They are entirely man-made but have been around long enough that particular styles are closely associated with objects, products, and companies. To learn more about this, I highly recommend checking out the research by Sarah Hyndman of *Type Tasting*. She's spent years creating fun experiments to understand people's associations with fonts, not just by how they look but also by how they might smell and taste. Based on that research, she has a great book called *"Why Fonts Matter."*

I never like to simply pick one font and roll with it. Instead, I select several that I feel could work well. I usually start with Adobe Fonts, where I'll enter the company name in the sample text field. I'll then browse the potential options, using filters if necessary. I try to find a font that feels appropriate to the goals and looks visually appealing. I note down and activate every font I think could work well.

Using Adobe Illustrator, I type the company name, change it to one of the fonts selected, then copy and update this as many times as needed to preview the name in all the selected fonts. After seeing all the options together, I then start to narrow it down to a handful of options based on the overall aesthetics and appropriateness.

When I have narrowed my options to one, I like to try different weights and adjust the tracking (the spacing between the letters) where needed until it looks perfect.

To speed this up, you might want to adopt the "font wall" method I learned from Jacob Cass of JUST Creative. To create your own, open a new Illustrator document, type any word, change the font to one you use frequently, then copy it and change the font to another. Keep doing this until you have added all your frequently used fonts, then save this as a template file. When you start a project, open this template document and use the 'find and replace' function to change the word to the company's name. This is a nice trick to quickly preview and test potential fonts.

To make fonts more distinct, I recommend modifying them or creating your own from scratch. Although, do this with caution. Typography design is a sophisticated art form. If the shapes are not perfect and optical adjustments have not been considered, the design will look amateur. To help you master your typography skills, I have listed some excellent books at the back of the book (see page 288).

CREATING A WELL-EXECUTED LOGO

Having a good idea is only the beginning. Ensuring the best execution will become a journey of experimentation and refinement.

As a starting point, I photograph the sketches I plan to develop further. I then place them into an Adobe Illustrator document, adding them into their own layer, which I lock. I then add a layer above this, where I start tracing the design or using it as a reference.

COPY & IMPROVE

The first tracing I do is usually rough. If I can quickly see the idea has potential once vectorised, I will begin to copy and improve the design to perfect it. I copy and edit the design multiple times to test and explore variations until I find the best execution of the idea. I ask myself:

- Can the design be simplified?

- Can anything be removed?

- Could a different layout work more effectively?

- How would the design look if it was chunkier or thinner?

- Are there any angles or shapes that could be consistent?

- What can I do to ensure the design works well in small sizes?

- Can the symbol use any stylistic elements from the wordmark for consistency?

Keep exploring until you've perfected the design.

THE USE OF GRIDS

If you've spent any time looking into logo design, you'll often see designs with grids applied to them, such as the Golden Ratio.

When I started out, I thought I also needed to use grids. While I still see the value in uniformity, I no longer use grids when designing a logo. Instead, I let the idea develop organically with no restraints.

Only once the design is at a point where I'm happy will I use shapes and lines to refine and perfect it; however, I often save that level of perfection until I know the design has been selected as it can be a time-consuming process. I go into that in more detail later in the book (page 134).

iCount

A Step Towards Safer Childbirth and Surgery

OPTICAL CORRECTIONS

When I started designing logos, I wanted everything to be as precise as possible. Despite the designs being mathematically correct, very often, there was something not quite right with my work. They just didn't look as professional as I would have liked.

My designs simply weren't on par with the work I had benchmarked myself against, and I couldn't work out what I was doing wrong… I felt my ideas were good, but the execution wasn't there.

That's when I met with an experienced designer who pointed out an error in my type design. He told me I needed to apply "optical corrections." Initially, I had difficulty seeing the issues he was highlighting, especially since I had aligned everything so carefully to a grid. But now, having an understanding of the intricacies of type design, the errors are in plain sight.

I thought that for a design to be perfect, it should align perfectly with a grid. However, that's not always the case. Our eyes like to play tricks on us, so for the design to look perfect to the human eye, sometimes we will need to modify the design based on what we see instead.

For example, back in 2015, Google released a new identity. They introduced a free-standing G symbol used across the company's social media profiles. Upon release, the overall reaction from the design community was a positive one, but there were a few people who carefully investigated the logo and pointed out what they believed were errors.

The Original

Using a Grid

Which looks better?

By applying shapes and lines over the symbol, they discovered it wasn't geometrically perfect. But if you were to attempt to fix those errors, you'll start to understand why the designer made those subtle imperfections.

If you apply a circle over the symbol, you will notice that the lower right side of the G has been pulled inwards slightly. This is to optically compensate for the missing part of the circle. Without this adjustment, the right side of the G appears to stick out a little too far. This tweak resolves that issue, ensuring that it looks correct to your eye, even though it's not geometrically precise.

It's intentional minor adjustments like this that help to perfect a design. When I discovered this, I noticed that the best designers and agencies apply various optical adjustments to almost every design, and it's that attention to detail that makes the designs so good. Once I started to use those observations in my designs, they also looked much more professional.

There are several optical adjustments that I've come across that I want to share. Most of these have come from the world of typography, but they are just as relevant when designing symbols.

OVERSHOOT

If you place a square next to a circle and make them precisely the same height, to our eyes, the circle will look like it's slightly too small. To compensate for this, you need to make the circle slightly larger, tricking our eyes into thinking it's the same height as the square.

This same illusion happens in typography. It's known as "overshoot," so you'll often notice that circular or pointed letters are usually taller than those that are more square.

When designing a logo, this illusion goes beyond typography. Since we often design with a combination of shapes, we need to consider their relationship and make adjustments where needed to ensure that shapes align optically rather than always being mathematically precise.

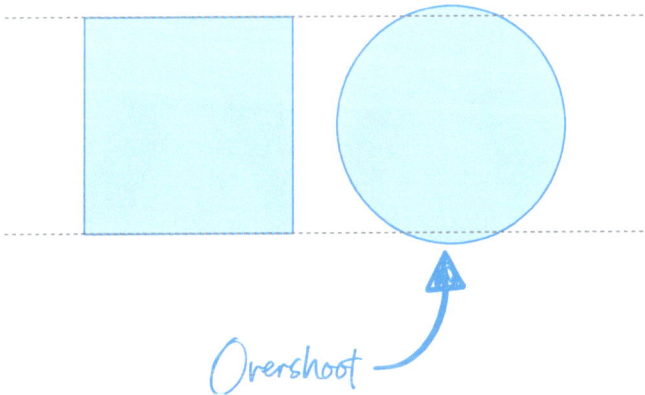

Overshoot

TAPERED INTERSECTIONS

If you draw an X or V and the strokes are kept the same consistent width, you will notice that where the shapes cross, such as the centre of the X and the lower part of the V, there will be a build-up of weight. To compensate for this, type designers will taper the shapes as they approach the intersection.

The same issue can happen with symbols and shapes; you'll want to use a similar method to solve the problem.

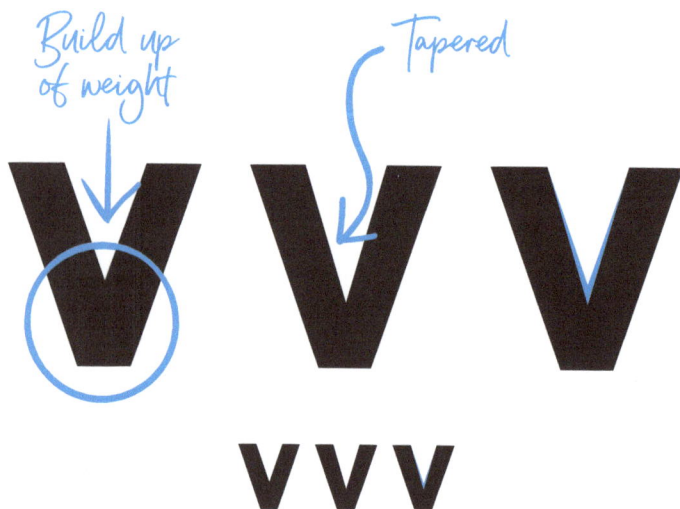

Build up of weight

Tapered

POGGENDORFF ILLUSION

For some reason, our brains have trouble processing angled lines partially covered by another shape. For example, if you overlap two lines of differing weights into an X shape, the thinner line will no longer look like it's straight. As you increase the angle, the illusion becomes more intense. This is known as the Poggendorff illusion. To accommodate for it, you'll need to slightly adjust the position of the line on either side so it looks optically correct.

This is commonly seen in typography design on letters such as X, Q, and an ampersand. However, when designing a logo with intersecting lines, you may need to accommodate for the illusion too.

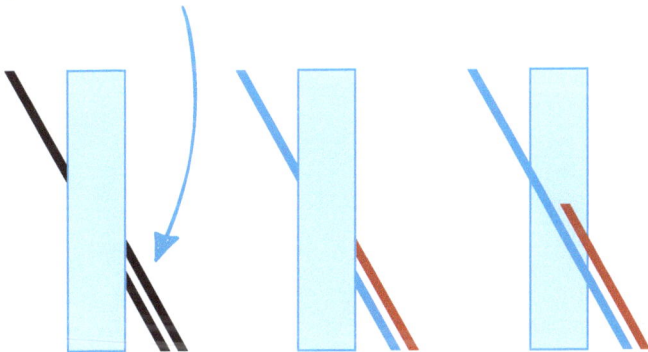

Which line looks correct?

Was it what you expected?

TRIANGLE-BISECTION ILLUSION

Imagine creating a play button, constructed using a circle, with a forward-pointing triangle in the middle. If you were to align the two shapes precisely, the triangle would appear out of place. You would need to move the triangle slightly to the right to make it look optically correct.

The same can happen when aligning any shape inside another. To ensure it looks right, make sure to align it optically.

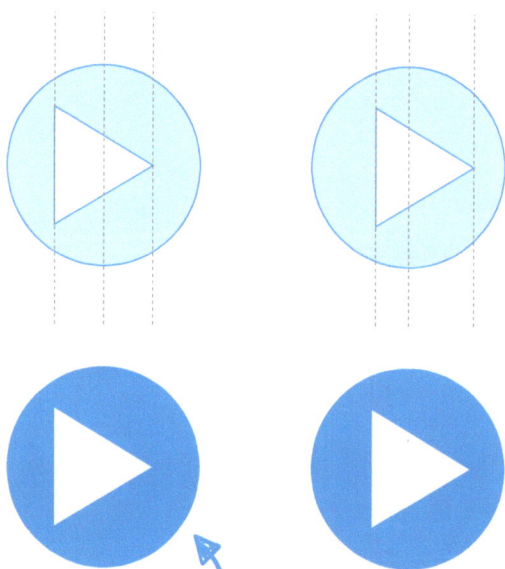

Precisely centred, but doesn't look it.

ANISOTROPIC CONTRAST

Imagine creating a letter L which has an overall consistent weight. Logic would assume you simply create a vertical stem and a horizontal bar using the same thickness.
But when you do that, our eyes like to trick us, and the horizontal bar weirdly looks heavier than the vertical. This is known as anisotropic contrast.

To resolve this, you need to peel away some weight from the horizontals until they look the same weight as the verticals.

This looks too heavy

GESTALT THEORY: CLOSURE

As the world around us is so complicated, our brain will attempt to simplify it by organising visual components into groups of "unified wholes." The physiological term to describe this is Gestalt theory.

There are several Gestalt principles, which include similarity, continuation, closure, proximity, figure/ground, and symmetry & order. These are useful to understand for all areas of design, so it's worth carrying out your own research. However, one I want to draw your attention to as a logo designer is the law of closure.

The principle is simple. If you draw the outline of a circle and then remove large segments of it, even though it has become many separate lines, our brains will fill in the gaps to see a single object. You see this principle leveraged frequently in the world of logo design. One of my favourite examples is the World Wide Fund for Nature panda logo. You'll notice that large chunks of the panda's outline are missing, but your brain doesn't have an issue filling in the missing parts.

IRRADIATION PHENOMENON

When designing a versatile logo, you'll want to create separate variants of the design for different situations. One of those is a white variant, which will be used on dark colours or images. Most people think all you need to do is change the colour to white, and you're done, but that's not always the case.

A weird illusion called the irradiation phenomenon can happen whereby the design's white parts look optically fatter than they should be. While it depends on the design, one quick solution that works in most cases is to apply a thin stroke, expand it, and then use the Pathfinder tool in Adobe Illustrator to remove it from the shape.

Exactly how much "weight" you scrape away will vary from design to design. It will need to be done by eye, and the aim should be to make the design look optically the same in white on black as it does in black on white. I find it helpful to put them next to each other to compare while doing this.

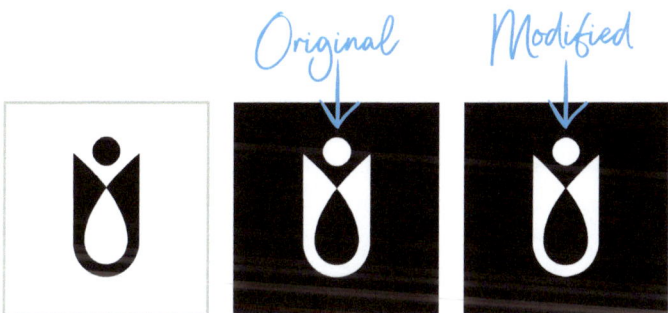

Original   *Modified*

CHOOSING COLOUR

Once I have the design to the point where it works effectively in solid black, I explore the use of colour. I like to keep colour to a minimum and often use just one or two colours in a logo, which I feel gives a more professional appearance. This has been influenced by observing the logos of the world's top 100 best-performing companies, which, with very few exceptions, use only one or two colours. However, this isn't a rule; it depends on the project goals. If it's appropriate to use multiple colours, I will.

Choosing exactly what colour(s) to use takes time. I try to find a balance between differentiation and the appropriateness of the meaning and feel of the colour.

The worst thing that can be done is to pick a colour already used by an established competitor. Doing so will cause confusion and likely have negative consequences for the client. For this reason, an essential first step is to study all competitors to understand which colours are already in use.

I like to visit the websites of all known competitors, screenshot the homepage, and place them into a large Photoshop file. Seeing everything together will allow me to identify which colours are already in use and which are "available" and can be owned by the client. That colour will need to remain appropriate, though.

If you're lucky enough that the available colours are appropriate to the client's business, then the choice will be an easy one. Sadly, the more competitive the market landscape, the harder it will be to create a completely fresh colour palette.

For industries where all colours have been used, which is common, I consider other colour tones not already in use, or even a combination of two or more colours that will allow for distinctiveness.

Aside from differentiation, I like to consider the colours' meaning too. Earlier in the book, I briefly discussed semiotics. Colour, by its nature, has all sorts of connections to culture, history, and objects.

There are also common meanings which we can consider when choosing a colour. For example, red relates to positive words such as beauty, energy, heat, passion, power, and love, as well as negative terms such as aggression, anger, danger, stop, and failure. Yellow, in comparison, relates to positive words such as fun, happiness, hope, joy, and optimism and negative words including jealousy, cowardice, caution, envy, and illness. A simple Google search and some common sense will determine the meanings of other colours.

The truth is that there is no right or wrong way to perceive colour. It really is a personal thing, but commonly perceived meanings will assist with design decisions and will help when presenting the designs.

It might just boil down to a completely subjective opinion from you or your client; however, try to find an objective reason first so that there's more to your design decisions than "I thought it looked good."

USING A COLOUR WHEEL

Unless I'm pairing with either black or grey, I'll use a colour wheel to help with my selection, so it's not simply a random choice. A colour wheel is a circular image showing a logically arranged sequence of colours.

Imagine first dividing a circle into three sections, coloured red, yellow, and blue. These primary colours can't be created by mixing other colours.

Imagine then adding colour between each of these, constructed using a mixture of the two on either side. These are known as the secondary colours: green, orange, and purple. Then, between these, we'll add the tertiary colours, which are yellow-orange, red-orange, red-purple, blue-purple, blue-green, and yellow-green.

A decent colour wheel will be broken down even further, as well as presenting shades and tints of each.

There are several colour combinations you can create using a colour wheel. These include **Monochromatic**, **Complementary**, **Analogous**, **Triadic**, **Tetradic**, and **Warm/Cool** colours.

MONOCHROMATIC

COMPLEMENTARY

ANALOGOUS

TRIADIC

TETRADIC

WARM/COOL

MONOCHROMATIC

A monochrome colour combination starts with a single colour and is made up of varying shades, tones, and tints of that colour. For example, orange, light orange, and a darker orange.

COMPLEMENTARY

Complementary colours are those found on opposite sides of the colour wheel. This combination creates the most substantial contrast, so they'll appear more vivid when placed side by side.

Complementary colours can be used if you want particular elements to stand out against the primary colour selected or to give depth to the design in some way.

ANALOGOUS

Analogous colours sit beside each other on the colour wheel. For the best results, I recommend choosing one prominent colour, then using the two beside it as accents within the design.

TRIADIC

Triadic colours are three colours that are evenly spaced on the wheel. To picture this, if you were to take an equilateral triangle and place it on the wheel, the colours at each point would make up the combination.

TETRADIC

Like the triadic combination, the tetradic colour combination is evenly spaced, but this time it uses four colours instead of three. To picture this, place a square over the wheel, then choose the colours at each corner.

WARM/COOL COLOURS

The colour wheel can also be divided into warm and cool colours. The warm colours are those from the reds through to the yellows. The cool colours are those from blue to green and purple. This can be particularly useful if you'd like to get across a certain feel or mood in the design.

Using the colour wheel as a guide, I'll explore several options until I find what I feel is the perfect balance of looking great and being appropriate and distinct.

Aside from using a colour wheel and the steps discussed in this chapter, I sometimes find online tools, such as coolors.co, useful for ideas and inspiration. More useful tools like this are listed at the back of the book (page 297).

It will take time to choose the perfect colour; however, investing your time will enable you to provide a thoughtful explanation to your client during the presentation.

THE USE OF GRADIENTS & EFFECTS

You may consider adding gradients and effects to your logo, but do so with caution, as they can often date quickly and can sometimes cause printing issues too, resulting in an unpleasant banding effect. If you're designing an identity for a digital environment, this becomes less of a problem.

AN IMPORTANT NOTE ON COLOUR GAMUT

Something you will need to be aware of is something called colour gamut, which refers to the range of colours a device can reproduce.

A digital device emits colour as RGB (red, green, and blue) light, which allows for the broadest possible gamut we can currently reproduce. Print uses CMYK (cyan, magenta, yellow, and black), which has a reduced gamut range compared with RGB. This means that not all colours you see on your computer can be reproduced in printed ink, which is most noticeable when dealing with very bright, vibrant, or neon colours.

To prevent issues, unless you're designing an identity that will only ever be seen and used in a digital environment, when selecting colour, I recommend switching your document colour mode to CMYK.

To learn more about colour, the best book I've read on the topic, which includes details on the cultural and psychological relationship with colour, is *Color Works* by Eddie Opara and John Cantwell.

DocFly

The Best Online PDF Editor

Create, Edit & Convert up to 3 PDF Files a month
for FREE with the best free pdf editor!

DocFly logo design by Ian Paget

LEARNING THE TOOLS

If you've gone through this section and are eager to experiment with logo construction, a fantastic learning exercise is to recreate excellent logo designs. While you should never directly copy, trace, or plagiarise design work, this can be a valuable exercise to assess your skills and become proficient with the tools.

Once you can confidently replicate designs with precision, challenge yourself by creating original designs to foster your creativity. A great idea that I've seen is to pick two words and visually combine them. This will allow you to apply many of the idea-generation processes discussed in this book, but with a much more simplified brief. You can use a dictionary or random word generator to help, but here are a few examples:

Rabbit + Flame

Mind + Coin

Window + King

Leaf + Star

Rocket + Learn

Frog + Luxury

Tree + Water

Car + Balloon

SET A BENCHMARK

Something I like to do in all areas of design is to find work that I consider the best and to use it as a benchmark. I recommend you do the same.

One of my all-time favourite books is *"Pentagram Marks."* It's a small book showcasing 400 symbols and logotypes meticulously crafted by Pentagram, renowned as one of the world's best design agencies. Sadly, this book had a limited print run of only 1,000 copies; however, if you're lucky, you can often discover affordably priced copies on eBay. Each logo featured in the book is remarkably simple, clever, and flawlessly executed.

Another book that presents a collection of inspiring logo design work is *"Identity,"* a monograph highlighting the creative journey of the design firm Chermayeff & Geismar & Haviv. Crafted by Standards Manual, this beautiful masterpiece of a book showcases logos that are not only visually striking but also crafted with exceptional skill.

By simply looking at work of this standard, learning from it, and applying the lessons to my own work, I'm steadily improving my craft.

There are plenty more designers and agencies that I look up to, so to help you discover your own benchmark work, I have listed a few of my favourites at the back of this book (page 303).

PART 6

PRESENT-ATION

WITH A SERIES OF CAREFULLY CONSTRUCTED LOGOS READY, I NOW CREATE A PRESENTATION TO SHOW THE CLIENT MY WORK.

IN THIS SECTION, I'LL SHARE WHAT I INCLUDE WITH TIPS AND ADVICE FOR PRESENTING THE WORK AND DEALING WITH ANY FEEDBACK.

PREPARING THE PRESENTATION

My approach to presenting logos has changed considerably over the years, and I've come to realise that it's the most critical part of the process.

When I started designing logos, I would put a few ideas together in a single image, number the options, and send it to my client for their thoughts. Regardless of how good the designs were, this almost always resulted in numerous rounds of revisions, ideas being "Frankensteined," and the end product being an embarrassment I'd never wish to share. Looking back, the reason that happened was caused by the way I presented the designs.

My approach today is very different, and as a result, clients trust my decisions, and I remain in control. Although I still like to show options, I now create a comprehensive presentation where I share each logo individually. This keeps the focus on each design without distraction and allows me to discuss my thought process and how I've successfully met the goals.

WHAT'S IN THE PRESENTATION?

I'm sure you're eager to hear how I present my designs to clients now, so let's jump right in...

The very first slide shows a title of the project, then before the first logo, I have a slide titled "Option 1."

On the following page, I then show the first logo…

I always start by showing a black-and-white version of the logo because colour can be very subjective. If someone dislikes a colour, they can quickly disregard the whole concept. However, by showing a single colour version first, I can focus on the overall concept without colour becoming a distraction. At the bottom right corner of this same slide, I like to show a small version of the logo to demonstrate that it also works effectively at small sizes. Then, on the following slide, I show the logo in colour.

I've met numerous designers who only present black-and-white options in their first presentation. They then explore colour options as a separate exercise once a direction has been agreed upon. In my experience, I've found that the average person struggles to visualise how a design might look once complete. Since colour can change the appearance of a design, I like to present what I feel would be the most appropriate colour scheme and explain the thought process behind the choice.

I also like to show inverted variants and, if the design allows it, different configurations, demonstrating that the logo is versatile and will work well in a wide range of applications.

A slide from the logo presentation for International Centre for Eye Health by Ian Paget

SHOW THE LOGO IN USE

A logo is unlikely to ever be seen in isolation on a white background, so on the following pages of the presentation, I show the logo in use on various items to help the client visualise how it might look in real-world use. I aim to show the logo in a range of sizes, and where possible, I create images relevant to the client's industry.

At larger sizes, I might show the logo on an exhibition stand or store exterior. At mid-sizes, show it on a business card or bag. Then at smaller sizes, I show it in the distance on a T-shirt or as an icon on a mobile device. Doing this shows how the logo will look in real use and how versatile it is too.

Showing the logo in use doesn't mean I need to spend money getting the logo printed on genuine items (although I have seen this done). Instead, it can be emulated using a range of tools. There are many "branding mockup" options out there, which I have listed at the back of this book (page 298); however, at the time of writing, I primarily use a mixture of LiveSurface, Placeit, and stock images.

LiveSurface is a plugin for Adobe Illustrator, which is only available for Mac users at the time of writing. It's directly integrated into Illustrator, meaning I can quickly and easily preview designs without leaving the Illustrator interface. The method is so quick and easy that I've made it my go-to application for testing and presenting designs, so it's totally worth the subscription cost.

Placeit is a subscription-based web application, with access to a wide range of items, including clothing, books, mugs, bags, business cards, and more. Once a mockup has been selected, I can simply upload an image of the logo, edit the colours, and preview the results on the website. Then, once happy, I can download a high-quality image (or even video) for use in the presentation.

If I can't find the perfect image in LiveSurface or Placeit, I'll resort to finding a suitable stock image and manually applying the logo using Photoshop.

I repeat the same format for each logo option, using the same mockup images. Then, on the final page of the presentation, I showcase all the designs collectively on a single page.

From time to time, before each design, I like to include a word, image, or series of images that help to explain the background of the concept being presented. For example, when I designed the logo for the International Centre for Eye Health, as mentioned earlier in the book, one of the ideas was a combination of an eye, the Earth, and an eclipse of the sun. So before presenting the logo, I shared three images that helped me to introduce the idea before the logo was revealed.

For a long time, I also included supporting notes alongside each design. This was to avoid design decisions being missed should my client share the presentation with others. Now I record a video to discuss my designs, which has been more effective. I discuss this in more detail shortly.

In most situations, I present options, but there have been several occasions when I've felt it appropriate to show just one logo. When I take this approach, I share more of the behind-the-scenes process, telling the story of how I came to this solution. I might share sketches, notes and images to show the journey, which helps my client to understand my thoughts, ideas and considerations, giving them confidence that the one logo presented is the perfect solution.

My presentation decks are designed in Adobe InDesign and then exported as a PDF; however, it could also be created in Illustrator, Keynote, or PowerPoint. To prepare this relatively quickly, I use a template. The first time I did a presentation, I dedicated time to perfecting it. Now I simply copy and edit a previous deck, allowing me to make the most of my time.

TIME TO SHOW THE CLIENT...

Now that the deck is ready, it's time to share it with the client. If you're anything like me, despite knowing that you've done your best, you may feel anxious before presenting design work. You've put in the hard work, and in the pit of your stomach, you may worry your client will reject the work… at least that's how I often feel.

Thankfully, after practicing this for several years and refining my presentation approach, this very rarely happens, so I hope the lessons I share in this book will help you to feel more confident, establish trust, and remain in control of the design phase.

I've approached presentations in a few ways, but in recent years I've found that the most successful approach has been to create a video. To record the video, I use Loom, which allows me to record my screen while I talk through my designs. Once I stop recording, it will automatically upload to the Loom website, where I can easily share it with my client. The video can then be watched by all the decision-makers at their convenience, and if needed, I can schedule a follow-up call to discuss it further.

Whatever your approach, avoid handing over your presentation without discussing your ideas. People are naturally curious, so they'll look through the designs, ignore any notes, and share them with colleagues, friends, and family. If you haven't discussed anything, they'll return with a list of subjective feedback, and you've lost control.

Once I hit the record button, the first slide shows the project title. At this point, I greet my client by name, let them know that the project has progressed well, that I'm excited to share the designs and set expectations of how many options I will present.

I then present each option, where I refer back to the project goals. This helps to demonstrate that I've put careful thought and consideration into every design decision.

Throughout the slides, I also stress the importance of a versatile logo. This is why I include a small version of the logo in the bottom right-hand corner, as this demonstrates how the logo is still clear and legible at smaller sizes.

When I progress to the mockups, I explain that a logo is never seen in isolation, as I have shown it so far, and by mocking it up on a range of items, the client can picture how the logo will look in real-world use. I start with the largest version and explain how the logo works effectively at large sizes. Then, as I progress, I show the logo in smaller sizes, highlighting how clear and legible it remains.

The presentation ends with a single slide showcasing all the designs discussed. At this point, I summarise the options, discussing each logo's pros and cons. I'll also suggest which option I believe is the most appropriate and why, while ensuring the client is aware that all options are viable and that I would never share anything that I feel is unsuitable.

If the video is recorded through Loom, I will end it by asking if they would like a follow-up discussion. Once the video has been uploaded, I send an email with a link to the video and a link to the presentation document, which I host on Dropbox, should they wish to take a closer look.

When I present in person, before sharing anything, I explain how and when I expect feedback. Nobody is taught how to give feedback, so if you don't do this, you can expect feedback to be given in a variety of ways. By setting rules from the outset, you remain in control and have done all you can to ensure feedback is structured and constructive.

Here's how the conversation might go: "All designs presented today have been created to fulfil the goals we agreed upon, so I refer to these during the presentation. Can I ask that feedback is left until all designs have been presented? That way, we can discuss them all together. I'd also like to encourage feedback to be given based on the goals. Don't worry about working out the solution; instead, let me know what's not right so I can find an alternative option."

Eternal Skol logo design by Ian Paget

It's fair to expect some feedback during the presentation, especially if the client is impressed. Keep an eye on this and make a mental note. Also, keep an eye on non-verbal communication, as you can get a lot of information from that. If they get carried away with the discussion, remind them that you will have a more detailed discussion at the end of the presentation.

"WHAT DO YOU THINK?"

Whatever you do, never ask, "What do you think?"
It's a project killer.

When I worked in an agency role, it was the responsibility of account managers to present my designs. Whenever someone new would join the team and it was time to show my work, "What do you think?" would almost always be a question they'd ask, and I'd want to cry, knowing that it would result in a long list of revisions.

While you need your client's approval, what they personally think of a piece of design is not the same as agreeing that you've successfully fulfilled the project goals. Stand by your decisions and explain how and why your logo design will succeed. This helps your client to trust you and have confidence that you're an expert.

When you ask "what they think," you've transferred the control to them. They'll share their personal thoughts and ideas, which is input that could be completely irrelevant. That's when you'll receive a list of subjective feedback and risk being treated like a puppet as your beautiful designs are ruined.

To prevent this in my agency role, when a new account manager joined the team, I'd book an introductory meeting with them. A crucial part of that meeting would involve me presenting a stapler to them in two different ways. First, I'd place the stapler down in front of them. I'd say, "I've designed a stapler. What do you think?"

What do you think?

They'd start looking at the stapler, and while there might be features they liked, they'd also be seeking out features they didn't like… ideas based on personal preference. "It's clunky. I don't like blue. I'd prefer it to be red. The mechanism is ugly." This happened because I asked them what they thought, so they provided their thoughts and ideas. They gave me what I asked for.

Then I present the stapler again. This time I talk through the features based on goals. I explain that it's easy to hold in one hand, effortless to staple twenty sheets of paper, easy to reload, and designed to be easily manufactured at a low cost per unit. I then ask, "Do you agree that this meets the goals of an office stapler?" This often results in a very clear yes.

This approach also sets the tone for feedback. If your design fails to meet the goals, you will receive constructive feedback that will help you find an alternative (often better) solution.

The two approaches have drastically different outcomes. The first approach means you come away with a list of changes, yet with the second, you come away with either an agreed design or helpful, objective feedback that will improve the design.

"What do you think?" is a question that can cause significant problems for designers. Sadly, it's the first question most people ask when presenting designs. Remove it from your vocabulary – asking this question will cause a slippery slope where you lose control of the designs.

DEALING WITH FEEDBACK

If you're lucky, the client will agree on a design right away, and you can proceed to finalise the artwork and prepare the files, which I discuss later in the book (page 152).

Sometimes, you may be given constructive feedback. Take note, update the designs, and schedule a follow-up meeting as required.

However, occasionally, you may be asked to make changes that you don't feel will work. In situations like this, I try to understand what the client is aiming to achieve with their suggested amendments, then if necessary, I will propose two alternatives: the first aligning with their request, and a second alternative that I feel solves the problem more effectively. Ultimately, it's up to the decision-maker which direction they take, but I provide as much advice and support as possible.

Sadly, from time to time, despite careful design decisions, you may encounter a client who simply does not like the designs, and they may also find it difficult to give clear feedback. Stay calm, listen to what they say, and work to find a suitable way forward. I often find it beneficial to ask a simple yet powerful question: "Why?" This usually helps to uncover the root of the problem.

BUT MY CLIENT STILL HATES THE DESIGN?

This can happen, so don't take it personally. If you've worked to understand the client, have agreed on a direction forward, and there's still no end in sight... You've done as much as you can. It sucks, but being prepared will save a lot of pain.

To protect from endless revisions and unreasonable treatment, I've added a couple of clauses to my contract. I'll discuss contracts in more detail later in the book (page 256).

The first relevant clause is to define the number of revisions within the project scope. A design never usually needs more than three revision rounds. Should that happen, the client has taken control, is guiding the design based on personal tastes, and the project goals have become irrelevant.

Defining the number of changes allowed within the project scope sets boundaries of what's expected. If I need to go above this without a clear direction forward and feel the client has become unreasonable, I have the freedom to choose if I want to proceed or if I want to part ways with the client.

It's a rare scenario, but sometimes parting ways is the best solution for both parties involved. To enable me to do this, I have a Suspension Policy in my contract allowing me to terminate the project. If I do this, the client doesn't need to pay the final 50% unless they plan to use any of my designs. The important thing is to learn from any negative experience. What could I have done differently? How can I prevent that situation in the future?

Take responsibility, even if it's the client's fault.

Nobody likes a bad client. Thankfully, there are some red flags you can spot during the sales process to help (hopefully) avoid working with unpleasant, demanding people. I discuss that later in the book (page 248).

Design is a challenge; however, if you work to understand the client's goals, design with intention, and explain your decisions effectively, you'll get approval almost every time.

ARE YOU ANXIOUS WHEN PRESENTING?

Presenting designs verbally can be daunting. It certainly was for me. In my school days, the mere thought of stepping in front of my class for a presentation would send waves of terror through me. I'd feel sick, have trembling hands, and stutter over my words. I went to great lengths to avoid such situations, often pretending to be ill.

However, in the professional world, public communication becomes an essential skill. Conquering this fear becomes not just a challenge but a necessity, especially if you aspire to have a successful career as a designer.

I struggled with anxiety well into my twenties, was later told I had social anxiety and sought therapy to help. If you find yourself in a similar situation as mine, where anxiety is hindering your progress, it's perfectly okay to seek support, just as I did.

Recognising that I had a problem and discussing it with my doctor was one of the best decisions I ever made. If you are dealing with anxiety, I wholeheartedly encourage you to take the same step.

Since the fear of public speaking is very common, I'd like to share a few tips that have assisted me in becoming a more confident speaker.

For starters, your posture makes a big difference. Most anxious people slouch. So put your shoulders back, your chest out, and sit up properly. Now breathe. Breathe in through your nose for six seconds and out through your mouth for four seconds. Doing this grounding exercise a few times while sitting correctly immediately calms me down before a presentation. The next thing is to practice as much as possible. I've done this in a couple of ways.

First, I attended public speaking classes. Many organisations help people improve their public speaking, such as Toastmasters. I'll openly admit that I didn't enjoy attending these classes, but it's a safe place to practise speaking to a group of people. The more you do it, the more comfortable you will become, and these groups are there to help.

The second way I practise is to record podcasts, both as a host and as a guest. This has helped me get comfortable speaking and improved my communication skills; plus, I'm reaching out to an audience in the process, which has additional benefits.

Overcoming any fear is never easy, and it will require you to work through it, but facing those fears will help you present more confidently and be more successful.

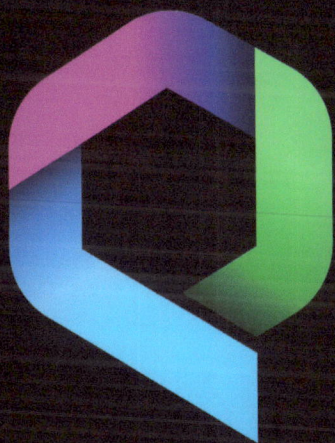

QUOTALL

www.quotall.com

Quotall logo design by Ian Paget

PART 7

FINALISING THE LOGO

BEFORE PREPARING THE FINAL FILES, I LIKE TO REFINE AND PERFECT THE DESIGN, ENSURING THE ARTWORK IS FLAWLESS. IN THIS SECTION, YOU'LL DISCOVER HOW I DO THIS.

REFINE & PERFECT THE DESIGN

Since I present several logo options, some designs will inevitably never be used. So the first time I show a logo, the artwork won't be 100% perfect. There may be minor imperfections that need to be fixed before I prepare the final logo package.

Getting a logo to the point of perfection can take several hours – even days – so only once my client has chosen a design will I work to get it to the point where it's as perfect as possible.

Let's dive into some of the exercises I carry out to perfect my designs.

USE SHAPES & LINES

When the logo contains a symbol or pictorial element, I like to refine and perfect it using shapes and lines. I aim to ensure that all curves are flawless and that the spacing and angles are consistent throughout. If required, I may even completely recreate the design.

At times, when the design requires it, I will inform my client of a second development stage. During this stage, I dive deeper into the chosen direction to achieve the best possible execution.

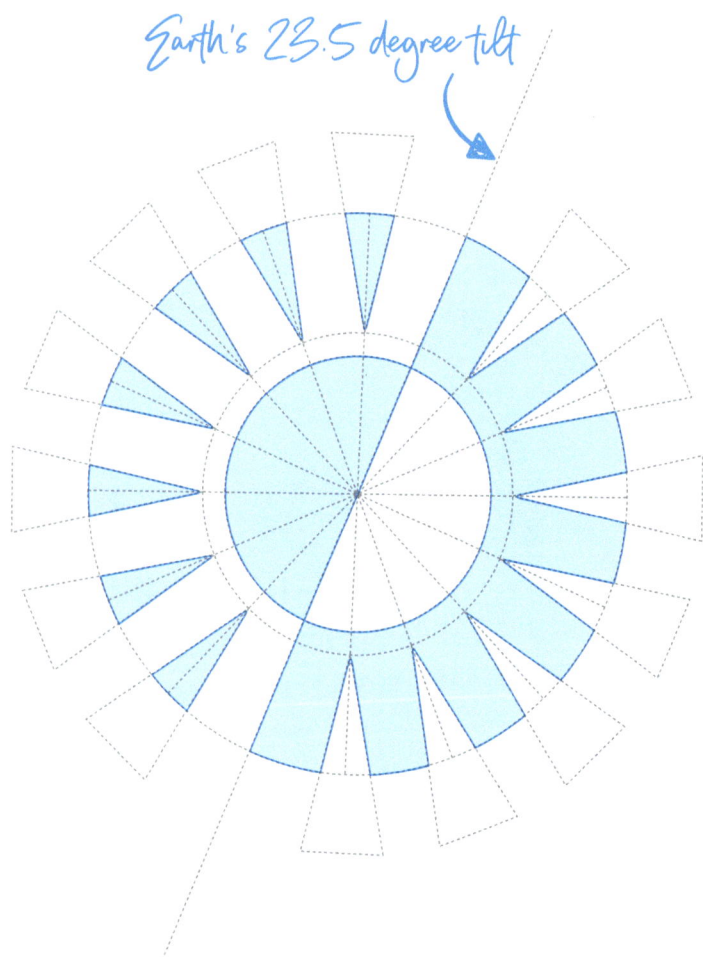

Earth's 23.5 degree tilt

Icon design, for International Centre for Eye Health
by Ian Paget, showing how lines and shapes were
used to assist with its construction.

The revised design may look slightly different from the initial presentation. If that's the case, I will share it with my client for approval before I prepare the final files.

PERFECT THE KERNING

When you type out a word and want to change the overall spacing between all the letters, you will adjust what's known as the tracking, and when you adjust the spacing of two individual letters, it's known as kerning.

When creating logos, since you're dealing with a limited number of letters in isolation, you'll often find it necessary to manually adjust kerning rather than relying on the default settings.

When I first started designing logos, I wanted everything to be mathematically perfect, so I would space out the letters so they had the exact same measurement between them. However, I quickly realised that this didn't look right, and after learning more about typography design, I learned that the kerning shouldn't consist of mathematically equal spaces, but instead "perceived equal spaces" between the letters… more of those optical adjustments again, as we discussed earlier!

Getting perfect kerning can take time to get your head around, although it's one of those small details that can make the difference between an amateur and a professional look, so mastering this skill is essential.

Some people like to imagine sand filling the spaces and work to make the volume of sand equal between each letter; however, I feel this can cause confusion with some letter combinations. Instead, I prefer to imagine the spaces filled with those water balloon snake toys I had as a kid, which paints a more accurate picture than sand, as they wrap around the inner parts of letters such as capital E's and S's rather than completely filling them.

It can become quite an art form. The key is understanding the spatial relationship between each letter, which will be a combination of straight, round, and diagonal edges. Two straight lines together will have the greatest distance between them; two curves together will have the least. A combination of a straight line and a curve falls somewhere in between.

Some letter combinations, such as a capital L and A, can be particularly troublesome because they leave large dead spaces. To solve this, the letters are sometimes joined to compensate for the large gap. Because there's not always a simple solution, I suggest adjusting the kerning of the problematic letters first and using that as a starting point to adjust the spacing of the other letters.

A helpful trick is to kern letters in groups of three, covering the rest of the design to help you focus. Some people also turn the logo upside down so that they see the letters as shapes rather than words, allowing errors to be more visible.

Before....

KERNING

Visibly wider gap here

...6 balloon snake toys applied...

KERNING

... and here's the final thing!

KERNING

To perfect everything, something I like to do, once I've determined the space between the shapes, is to draw little squares, which I use as spacers to make sure all the spacing between similar shapes is consistent throughout the logo.

A great way to master your kerning skills is to play the Kerning Game, which you can find here: type.method.ac

OUTLINE FONTS

If you have any text within the design that's still editable, you'll want to convert it to shapes (or "outlines").

To do this in Adobe Illustrator, use the Direct Selection tool to select the live text, then from the main menu, choose Type, then Create Outlines.

Doing this will ensure your client won't need the font installed on their computer to use the logo, and you'll be confident that your design will always look great.

EXPAND STROKES

If your design includes any strokes, if they are left "live," and someone scales your logo, the strokes will maintain the line weight instead of scaling proportionately, which will ruin your design. To avoid this issue, you must "Expand" the strokes so they become shapes. To do this, select the shapes, then from the main menu, hit Object, then Expand.

You'll also want to do the same with any effects you've applied. In this case, you'll first need to "Expand Appearance," which will permanently apply the effect.

As a side note, I recommend keeping a backup copy of your logo with all the editable live elements. This precaution ensures that you have it available in case any updates are required.

MERGE SHAPES

If your design consists of multiple overlapping shapes of the same colour, merge them into one unified shape using the Unite option in the Pathfinder Panel.

FIX BROKEN PATHS

When building shapes, sometimes you can unknowingly end up with open paths.

A handy way to see this is to change the view mode to "Outlines." To see your artwork in this mode, select View from the main menu, then choose Outlines from the dropdown. To revert, select View once again from the menu, then select Preview.

To rejoin the paths, select the two endpoints using the Direct Selection tool, then from the menu, select Object > Path > Join or use the keyboard shortcut Ctrl+J on Windows or Cmd+J on Mac.

REMOVE REDUNDANT ANCHOR POINTS

After outlining fonts and expanding objects, you'll often find that shapes have more anchor points than are needed. So that the artwork is as clean as possible, I remove any points that are not essential.

Although Illustrator has some inbuilt tools for reducing points, I use a feature included in Astute Graphics, a plugin that extends the software's capability. With their "Smart Point Removal Brush," you can simply brush out unwanted points, making the whole process effortless.

ZOOM IN

To perfect the artwork, I recommend zooming in closely, which will help you spot and fix any imperfections.

CREATE LOCKUPS

Once you've perfected your logo artwork, now is the best time to create different configurations of your design, known as lockups.

Usually, if there's a separate symbol and wordmark, I do a version with the symbol to the left of the wordmark. I also do a second "stacked" variant where I position the symbol above. On some occasions, if the design warrants it, I may create additional configurations that allow for greater flexibility. For example, a fashion brand might want multiple variants that can be used across its clothing line.

Sky High Sports logo design by Ian Paget

Do be aware that adding more lockups can confuse your client, so I always like to have a default option and provide supporting guidelines.

CREATE COLOUR VARIANTS

I will now prepare various colour formats for each version of the logo, including full-colour, black, white, and inverted.

FULL-COLOUR VERSIONS

The most obvious version of the logo will be the full-colour version.

It's important to note that the colours may not appear accurately if your monitor isn't calibrated correctly. To ensure the utmost accuracy in your colour selections, you may want to take a Pantone-first approach.

Standard colour printing uses a four-colour process known as CMYK, which stands for Cyan, Magenta, Yellow and Black. These four colours are layered using tiny dots to create a wide range of colours. However, the layering of colours in this process can cause slight variations between print runs. While most people may not notice these differences, it can be an issue if you require an exact and consistent colour across all printed materials.

To address this, one solution is to establish a single spot colour. For consistent colour reference, the universally recognised Pantone system comes into play. If your logo is printed using Pantone inks, the colour will remain consistent regardless of where the printing is done, as long as the same paper stock is used.

The downside with Pantone is that there's usually an increased cost to the production run, so most people will resort to CMYK printing. This is fine in most cases, but providing a CMYK and a Pantone version of the final logo is good practice.

I usually initially select colours using CMYK. I then choose the closest matching Pantone colour. If you want to have the most consistent overall colour, choose the Pantone colour first, and from that, you can work out the CMYK, RGB and Hex colour codes.

For accuracy, use a Pantone swatch book, and don't rely on automatic colour conversion or pick the colours based on what you see on your screen.

Pantone swatch books are expensive, however, using them to check colours ensures that your choice is accurate, so it's a worthwhile investment. I recommend getting a set of Pantone Colour Bridge books, which show the Pantone colour compared to its closest CMYK variant, along with the RGB and hex colours in one place. Coated and uncoated colours can sometimes differ significantly, so I recommend having both coated and uncoated books and selecting the colours manually under good lighting conditions.

BLACK VERSIONS

Along with full-colour versions of the logo, I will also provide single-colour variants. This is so that the logo can be easily produced in situations such as single-colour printed documents, promotional merchandise, embossing, laser-cutting, vinyl-cut signage etc.

If the logo comprises of multiple objects, before changing it to black, I merge the shapes to form one object, then remove any redundant points.

Occasionally, it might not be as simple as selecting the logo and changing its colour to black. I might need to modify the design slightly so that it looks as close to the full-colour design as I can achieve in a single, solid colour.

WHITE VERSIONS

I also provide white versions too, that can be used on coloured backgrounds or over dark images.

This can often be created by changing the black version to white, but it occasionally needs special attention.

Earlier in the book, I described an optical illusion called irradiation phenomenon whereby the white parts of the design look optically larger than they should be when placed on a dark colour. If required, this can be solved by slicing off thin layers from the design, as described.

If the design includes a face or eyes, creating white variants will be a little more challenging. What should be a highlight is now black, and what should be a shadow is now white, so the design looks like a negative.

There are countless ways to fix this, and the chosen method will depend on the design. One great example of this is the Premier League logo, created by DesignStudio. In the white variant, they have created the lion's face as a separate object, allowing it to remain white, and framed the lion's mane with a white outline.

Left: Premier League Logo single-colour version in black. Right: A white variant.

Interestingly, the two designs were later consolidated into a single version. This decision is understandable considering the scale of the organisation as it's likely individuals without design backgrounds were using the incorrect file in inappropriate situations, so this simplified everything. This is a factor worth considering if you expect a large audience using the logo.

INVERTED VERSIONS

If the design allows for it, I also like to include a full-colour inverted variant, modified to work well on a background of the primary logo colour, or black rather than white.

This is usually as simple as changing anything in the design that uses the primary colour to white. However, there may be instances where I will need to modify the design slightly, as I do with white versions of the logo.

SPECIAL CASES

The colour formats described above will suffice for most projects, but occasionally, there might be special cases where you need to create further variants.

One example I frequently prepare is a gold foil variant, where one of the colours is replaced with a shiny foil for a luxurious look and feel. In these cases, I will add a spot colour to the artwork in a colour that's not used in the design, such as a bright pink or green, which I will name "Gold Foil." By doing that, when the logo is printed, that spot colour can be replaced with gold foil.

SIZING THE LOGOS

One of the final steps I like to take before preparing the kit of files is to resize the logos.

As the files use vectors, meaning they can be scaled up and down without losing quality, technically, the size of the final files doesn't matter. However, I like to size them so that if they are placed into an InDesign document, they are already appropriately sized.

To ensure they are the intended size, I like to set up an A4 artboard and then scale the logos to the size I want them to appear on the page. There's no exact science to this; I simply go by what looks good.

Now that's done, we're ready to prepare the final kit of logo files!

Shark Bite 2 logo design by Ian Paget

PART 8

PACKAGING THE LOGO FILES

ONCE I HAVE PERFECTED THE DESIGN AND CREATED ALL THE VARIANTS, I WILL NOW PREPARE A FINAL LOGO PACKAGE.

IN THIS SECTION, YOU'LL DISCOVER WHAT FILES I SAVE, HOW THEY'RE NAMED & HOW I SEND THEM.

PREPARING THE FINAL PRODUCT

Once I have perfected the design and created all the variants, I will prepare a package of logo files. This package will be the final product, ready to be sent to my client upon receipt of the final payment.

In the past, I would spend hours manually preparing all the files. However, I've significantly streamlined this process by using an Adobe Illustrator extension called Logo Package Express, created by my friend Michael Bruny-Groth, which allows me to generate and organise the files automatically within a matter of minutes.

You can purchase Logo Package Express by heading to **logogeek.uk/extension** (This is an affiliate link, so I'll receive a small commission if you buy the product using this link, so as a thank you, if you use promo code LOGOGEEK you'll get an additional 20% off).

Not everyone will want to use this, or you might be using alternative vector software, so let's dive into the files I prepare and how I send them.

THE FILES

PRINT FILES

The print files will be in vector format, which can be scaled to any size without losing quality. As they're for print, they will be in CMYK colour mode.

Your client will need these files if they want to get anything professionally printed or want design work carried out, such as brochures, leaflets, exhibition stands, vehicle printing, pens, etc.

Here's a summary of the different print files I include:

- **AI** – an AI file is the original editable Adobe Illustrator working file.

- **PDF** – PDF files, which stands for Portable Document Format, can be universally viewed on any computer with Adobe Acrobat (or another PDF viewer). It's also possible to preserve Illustrator editing capabilities when saving in this format, meaning it can be opened and modified like an AI file.

- **EPS** – EPS format, which stands for Encapsulated PostScript, is a vector file that can be opened by the broadest range of software, including older versions of Illustrator and software outside of the Adobe family. For this reason, your client may be asked to supply this format to print or manufacturing companies.

DIGITAL FILES

Digital files are for electronic use in various situations, including websites, presentations, social media and email signatures. These will be in RGB colour mode.

Here's a summary of the different digital files that I supply:

- **JPG/JPEG** – JPG format, which stands for Joint Photographic Experts Group, are most commonly seen online. This is because the format provides excellent image compression, so the file size is small and will load quickly.

- **PNG** – PNG format, which stands for Portable Network Graphics, allows for transparency, so these can be placed over coloured backgrounds or images.

- **SVG** – SVG files, which stands for Scalable Vector Graphics, is a vector image format that can be used digitally. With higher-resolution screens now common place, an SVG file will ensure the logo remains sharp no matter what device it's viewed on.

JPG and PNG files are raster-based files, meaning that they will become pixelated or appear blurry if your client scales the image above its intended size. For this reason, I supply a range of sizes. These images are set to 72 DPI, which will work for the majority of purposes while keeping the file size low.

There are no set rules for the sizes you supply, but for JPG and PNG files, I like to provide large, medium and small versions of each logo, and the size is based on how I commonly see the files being used.

Northumberland logo design by Ian Paget

For example, the largest is sized to fit a common screen resolution, which at the time of writing is 1920 × 1080 pixels, allowing the logo to be used full screen within a presentation. For the medium size, I take it down to 50% of this. The smallest is then sized to fit an email signature, so scaled down to around 200 pixels wide, which may vary based on the design.

NAMING THE FILES

When saving the files, it's important to give them descriptive names so that the client can easily identify each file. I follow a straightforward naming convention for this purpose:

[Company-Name]-Logo-[Colour]-[Colour-Mode]-[Size] *(Note that size is only relevant to the raster-based files, JPEG and PNG).*

Take Joe's Burgers for example, if the logo is full colour, and I save the vector print files, the file name will look like this: Joes-Burgers-Logo-Full-Colour-CMYK.ai

Using the same example, if I save the largest version of the PNG file, it might look like this: Joes-Burgers-Logo-Full-Colour-RGB-1920px.png

I'll use another example so it's clear. This time the company name is Sterilight. If the logo is a full colour; Pantone-coated version, the file name will be: Sterilight-Logo-Full-Colour-Pantone-Coated.ai

KETO COLLAGEN

↑↓ NOW KETO

KetoCOLLAGEN™
VANILLA CREME

Dietary Supplement
Net Wt. 11.57oz (328g)

KETO COLLAGEN

↑↓ NOW KETO

KetoCOLLAGEN™
STRAWBERRY CRÈME

Dietary Supplement
Net Wt. 11.2oz (320g)

KETO ENERGY

↑↓ NOW KETO

Keto ENERGY™
BLUEBERRY BLAST

Dietary Supplement
Net Wt. 11.3oz (318g)

MCT OIL POWDER

↑↓ NOW KETO

MCT Oil Powder
SALTED CARAMEL

Dietary Supplement
Net Wt. 11.25oz (319g)

EXOGENOUS KETONES

↑↓ NOW KETO

Boost PureBHB™
CHOCOLATE SEA SALT

Dietary Supplement
Net Wt. 7.46oz (219g)

MCT OIL POWDER

↑↓ NOW KETO

MCT Oil Powder
UNFLAVORED

Dietary Supplement
Net Wt. 10.56oz (300g)

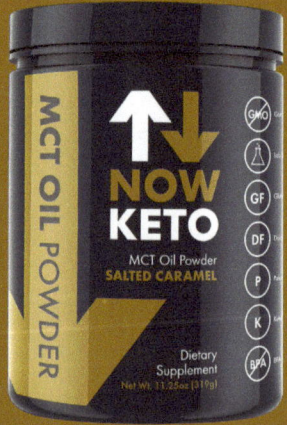

Now Keto logo and packaging design by Ian Paget

ORGANISING THE LOGO FILES

You've created a lot of different files, now you need to properly organise them.

I put the files from each lockup into a folder of its own, and then within that, I have four separate folders: Full Colour, Inverted, Black, and White. Inside each of these, I'll have a Digital and a Print folder where the appropriate files will be stored.

The full-colour print folders are further organised into subfolders, including CMYK, Pantone Coated, and Pantone Uncoated.

As there are so many files, to help my clients, I also like to include a single-page PDF document that explains all the file formats. For larger projects, this PDF might be a more in-depth branding guidelines document that includes fonts, colours and more.

Once the files are complete and organised, I compress them into a Zip file and they're ready to send.

Orema logo design by Ian Paget

SENDING THE FILES

Before sending the files, I ensure that I've been paid in full.

I used to send the files as soon as they were complete and provide the invoice simultaneously. But this caused problems. The client has received the final product, so there's no longer an incentive to pay.

Even trustworthy clients would take their time. On one occasion, the final payment was never made! The client ghosted me and started using the logo, so I needed to go through the small claims court process to get paid, which was a nightmare!

When you transfer the files upon receipt of payment, as the client is excited to start using them, they will always pay quickly.

Once the invoice is settled, I then transfer the files.

There are endless ways to store and send files, but I personally use Dropbox, which I also use to keep a backup of my computer. I like to write a friendly email to my client, and then from Dropbox, I copy the download link and apply that to the email so the files can be easily downloaded. If I don't hear back from my client within a few days, I check to see if they have downloaded the files, and if they have any questions I answer them.

As the files are now sent and the project complete, I ask for a testimonial, which I ask to be added to my Google business page. I can also share this within case studies or showcase it across social media, which helps to build credibility for potential future clients.

PART 9

IMPORTANT LEGAL STUFF

DESIGNS ARE PROTECTED BY COPYRIGHT & TRADEMARK LAW, MEANING YOU CAN'T JUST DESIGN ANYTHING YOU WANT.

IN THIS SECTION YOU'LL DISCOVER HOW TO CHECK IF YOUR LOGO IS ORIGINAL & IF IT CAN BE REGISTERED AS A TRADEMARK. YOU'LL ALSO LEARN ABOUT FONT LICENSING.

TRADEMARK LAW

Companies invest large sums of money promoting their company, product or service and will do all they can to protect their intellectual property, especially their logo. That means you must have an understanding of copyright and trademark law so you don't unintentionally get your client in any legal trouble or get in a sticky situation yourself.

In most countries, including the UK, EU and US, you automatically get copyright protection for any design you create and that prevents others from using your designs without permission. Copyright law, however, doesn't stop somebody else from using a similar design to identify their business, and that's where trademark law comes into play.

When you register a logo under trademark law, it becomes protected and discourages other businesses from adopting a "confusingly similar" design. Once the logo has been registered, the ® symbol can be added to the logo, and a business can legally protect its identity should another company have a similar-looking logo.

Until a logo is registered, you cannot use the ® symbol on the logo. You can, however, include the TM symbol on any logo to show intended ownership in advance of and during the trademark registration process. There's no exact rule about the size and placement of these symbols, but you usually see them at the top right corner of the logo.

Trademark registration isn't something I offer my clients. Although, if they express an interest in this area, I refer them to a trademark attorney.

IS MY LOGO IDEA ORIGINAL?

Now you know more about copyright and trademark law, hopefully, you've realised that you can't design anything you want. This leads us to ask ourselves the question: "Is my logo idea original?" This isn't an easy question to answer, so I will break it down into two questions: "Does a logo need to be original?" and "How do I check if my logo design infringes on any existing trademarks?"

DOES A LOGO NEED TO BE ORIGINAL?

Since a logo identifies a business, in an ideal world, every logo we create should be distinct and original. But when it comes to simple marks, almost everything that can be created has probably been created. The odds of you unintentionally designing something remotely similar to something already in existence is high.

If you become obsessed with the idea of creating something that's 100% new, you'll never come up with a single idea and be crippled with anxiety. To overcome this pressure, instead of aiming to create a completely original logo, I focus on differentiating it from the competitive landscape in which it will be used.

This doesn't mean you can copy or steal ideas, and it shouldn't be an excuse to be lazy, but as long as you're creating ideas of your own and you've worked to help the business stand out in the competitive landscape, you're unlikely to face issues.

When a logo goes through the trademark registration process, it will be assigned to one or more business categories. The more categories you add, the higher the cost. Because of this, most companies will only ever register the logo in the categories associated with their business. This means that a plumber and a dance school could have similar logos, but as there's no conflict, there's no risk of confusion.

The Nike and Sure Deodorant logos help to explain my point. Both are stylized ticks. As they are in very different industries, there's no conflict of interest and no confusion. You may not even have noticed the similarity yourself. If, however, Sure decided to start making sports clothing, I'd imagine Nike's legal team would be on their case.

Nike logo

Sure Deodorant logo

Since we're talking about originality, do you think Nike and Sure were the first companies to use a tick in their logo? Unlikely. But they were probably the first in their competitive landscape to use them.

My point is not to be overly harsh on yourself. Work to create something original and unique within the competitive landscape, then do your due diligence to check you're not unintentionally infringing on any existing trademarks, which I discuss next.

HOW TO CHECK IF THE LOGO INFRINGES ON ANY TRADEMARKS

The only way to know for certain that your logo doesn't infringe on any existing trademarks is to consult with a Trademark Attorney. However, you can do your due diligence and take steps to get a good indication the logo you've designed will very likely be protectable without issue.

Here's the most comprehensive method I've encountered, which I learned from my friend, Col Gray at Pixels Ink.

Begin by using the reverse image search functionality across a range of search engines, including Google, TinEye, and Yandex. Drag and drop the logo you have designed into each to see if anything similar comes up in the search results. This will highlight any potential copyright infringements and similar logos already registered.

To do a more formal check, head to wipo.int/branddb. This is the Global Brand Database of the World Intellectual Property Organisation (WIPO), where you can check globally registered names and logos.

Once on the WIPO website, if you navigate to the Image tab, you can search the database using an image in a simple three-step process. The first step is to upload an image of your logo.

Trade Mark Wizards logo design by Ian Paget

On the next step, you'll need to filter your search by Concept, Shape or Colour. If you select Concept, the search will use AI to find similar concepts. If you choose Shape, the search will find designs with similar lines distributed throughout the image and ignore colour. If you select Colour, it will search for designs with similar colours throughout the image.

On the last step, you will choose either Verbal, Non-Verbal or Combined. Select Verbal if your design includes only text; select Non-Verbal if you're uploading only a symbol; select Combined if your logo uses a combination of type and image. Now select the filter button to be presented with results.

Hopefully, you won't come across anything too similar, however, if you find something almost identical or exactly the same, even if it's in a different category, it will be worth steering in a slightly different direction to avoid any potential issues for your client. If you're ever unsure, consult with a trademark attorney.

As an extra layer of comfort, I've developed a professional relationship with a trademark firm that provides me with an infringement opinion. While this still doesn't guarantee the logo can be trademarked, since an expert has made an informed assessment, it's unlikely that any issues will arise during the registration process.

Doing this can take a little time, but it's worth doing the necessary due diligence to ensure your client can safely own and protect the logo you've designed.

FONT LICENSING

Font licensing can be particularly confusing when you're new to design, however, I hope to provide more clarity.

Fonts are like software, meaning that when you buy a font, you don't actually own it. Instead, you have purchased a licence to use it.

To create the logo, you, as the designer, need to own a licence. Once you convert the font to outlines, it's no longer a font, so your client doesn't need a licence to use the logo. They only need to buy a licence if the font will be installed on their computer(s) and used for additional design elements.

This means you cannot send a font file to your client or anyone else. If they want to use the font commercially, they will need to purchase their own licence. If it's a free font with a commercial licence, you don't need to worry.

PART 10

ATTRACT CLIENTS

TO MAKE A LIVING DESIGNING LOGOS, YOU MUST SUCCESSFULLY ATTRACT PAYING CUSTOMERS.

IN THIS SECTION, I SHARE HOW I'VE CONSTRUCTED A PORTFOLIO WEBSITE & MY EFFECTIVE MARKETING STRATEGIES FOR CONSISTENTLY GENERATING LEADS. ADDITIONALLY, I SHARE ADVICE TO HELP YOU STAND OUT FROM THE CROWD.

SHOW YOUR WORK

By now, you should have an understanding of what makes a good logo and the creative process behind creating them. However, to make a living as a logo designer, once you've honed your skills, you need find and attract clients.

Your first paying client will likely come from your existing network, which includes friends, family, and colleagues.

Be proactive in informing everyone you know that you're now designing logos and looking for projects. Put an announcement on every social channel, personally message everyone on your contacts list, and mention it when catching up with friends and family. The more people who know what you're doing, the higher the odds are that someone out there will reach out for your support.

Most people won't buy anything unless they can see what they're buying. That's the case for most industries, and it's even more essential if you're a designer. People need to see proof. Your previous work examples, experience and reputation, is that proof, and that will become your most important asset as a designer.

You need to show your work, and the best way to do that is within a portfolio. There are several ways to create a portfolio, however, I highly recommend to build a website to display your work.

WHY YOU NEED A WEBSITE

It was only after I created a website to showcase my work that I began attracting clients. The more I worked on that website, the bigger and better the opportunities became. But I'll be honest… my first website wasn't very good.

I never had the intention of Logo Geek becoming a business. Since I had an active full-time Design Director role, I was treating my logo design side hustle as a hobby. My website was built for fun and intended as a simple gallery where I could store my designs and document what I was learning. I made it for me.

I had unintentionally created a public space where people could see my work, my passion for design and know where to find me. After sharing it on social media, I unexpectedly had old acquaintances, including distant school friends and former colleagues, reach out seeking assistance with their logo projects.

I added new designs to the website as I completed them, along with case studies and testimonials. I also wrote blog posts, including those sharing the behind-the-scenes development of the designs. There was no intentional plan, as it was something I enjoyed as a hobby; however, this started to attract enquiries from business owners outside my current network.

Online platforms, such as Instagram, Behance and Dribbble also allow you to show off what you can do quickly and easily, but if you intend to make a living from logo design, I would caution against entirely relying on any of these platforms. This is because you don't control the experience. At any time, the platform can change or even disappear altogether.

More importantly, while you can point a potential client to your profile to show off your work, you must be aware that you've also sent them to a platform full of work from a global community of designers. Your client, who may never have met another designer, can now easily browse the work of other designers who may be more talented and cheaper than you.

In comparison, you have complete control of the layout, content, images and experience when you build a website. When prospective clients land on your website, they are in your world. You're the only designer in the room. Since it's your platform, you can showcase your knowledge and experience in a way nothing else can. If the client likes your work and trusts your capabilities, then they become yours for the taking.

This doesn't mean you shouldn't use any social platforms or gallery websites though. They should instead be treated as marketing tools to supplement your website.

DECIDING ON A NAME

Before building a website, you will need to decide on a name. The direction you can go falls into two general categories. Either you operate under your own name, or you create a business name. Each has pros and cons, but the ultimate decision will be based on where you want to take the business in the long term.

At this moment in time, I'm content working on my own and have no immediate plans to build a team. If you share the same outlook, you can choose to simply use your name. When it comes to website addresses, most designers simply register their full name as their domain, such as ianpaget.com, which I own, although, some opt to incorporate their first or last name followed by the word "designs."

However, it's important to note that this approach has its downsides. Because the business is closely tied to you and your personal brand, it may be challenging to sell in the future. Also, if you ever decide to expand and grow a team, the name might not be as suitable, although it has worked for some in the past.

The other option is to create a business name. If you plan to build a team and create an agency, this is the direction you'll want to take. You can of course take this direction as a solo business too, as I have done with "Logo Geek."

There was no clever strategy behind the name I selected. My business was a hobby, so I simply wanted "logo" to be in the name and for the website domain to be available. Things have changed since then, as more domain names have become available, but at the time, my choice was between either a UK or an international dot com domain.

Today, thankfully, plenty of newer website domains are available, such as ".design," which has an abundance of great options available for the taking.

Sterilight Robots logo design by Ian Paget

Although it wasn't my first choice, when I discovered that the UK domain for Logo Geek was available, I registered it immediately. As my business has grown, I've also secured the .com address, all the social media handles, and registered the name as a trademark too. This didn't happen overnight. It took time, money, and perseverance (especially to secure the Twitter/X handle). However, I now own the Logo Geek name and can protect it.

Although I've achieved success with Logo Geek, if I were to start everything from scratch, my approach to naming would be much more strategic. I would consider the type of clientele I want to attract and create a name that directly resonates with those individuals. I would also consider a name that doesn't include the word "logo" so that I can shift my service offering in any direction I wish. With the name Logo Geek, there's an expectation that I design logos, and only logos.

As with anything, you learn from your experiences. Nothing is stopping me from pivoting and starting anew, so whatever you decide, you'll always have the freedom to change it in the future. That's the beauty of working for yourself. Thankfully, I'm still obsessed with logo design.

Name creation isn't easy, so I have listed several useful resources at the back of this book (page 309).

Once you've decided on a name, I recommend registering and securing your preferred website address, which you can do through services such as GoDaddy, 1&1, and 123-Reg.

BUILDING A WEBSITE

I appreciate that building a website can be daunting for anyone new to it. That's why I want to stress that your first website doesn't need to be perfect. Keep it simple. I've met several young designers who dream up extravagant website designs with animations and effects, which is a great long-term plan, but from day one, it's not needed. The more complicated your goals, the longer it will take to make progress.

I started my career designing for print, so once a design was complete and printed, that was it and there was no going back. When designing for the web, anything built can easily be changed or added to. Start with a simple website that includes only the most essential elements, then over time, make updates and build upon them.

Although my first website was imperfect, it contained everything needed – examples of my work, process, story and contact information.

I built what I describe as a "minimum viable website," a very basic website as a starting point. Picture it as a simple one-page website displaying six examples of my designs, a brief bio about me, and my contact details. It was so simple that I could put it together in just a few hours. As time passed, I gradually added more pages and content, such as portfolio examples with in-depth case studies, additional content about me and my story, a process page, FAQs, testimonials, a contact page, and helpful information within a blog... The list can go on and on.

Building an in-depth website won't happen overnight, so if you take this route, don't try to do it all in one go. Start simple. Begin attracting clients. Then let everything take shape one small step at a time.

As it's a big topic and not the focus of this book, I won't delve into this subject in great detail. However, to assist you on your journey, I will point you towards a few website builder platforms I have personally used and can recommend.

SQUARESPACE

If you're new to building websites, SquareSpace.com is an excellent place to start. They have a wide range of great-looking templates and you can build pages in a relatively intuitive drag-and-drop interface. There's also plenty of training material and support out there.

WORDPRESS

If you want greater capability and control, look into WordPress, which is how I built my first website.

If you're new to website design, you might not be aware that most websites have a back-end system that allows you to manage all the content. This is called a "content management system" (CMS). WordPress is an open-source CMS, meaning that it's free to use and modify, so it's become one of the most popular, with millions of websites built using the platform. Note that there are two versions: wordpress.com and wordpress.org. I am referring to wordpress.org, which is the self-hosted version.

uGlow ageless tanning water hydrates your skin, developing your glow.

HOW TO USE:
Simply spritz on the skin, for best results gently blend using uGlow tanning application mitt & brush.

ADVICE:
This product does not contain any SPF, always protect your skin against natural UV Rays. Best kept in a cool dark place. For external use only. Avoid contact with eyes.

INGREDIENTS:
AQUA, DIHYDROXYACETONE, ERYTHRULOSE, METHYLPROPANEDIOL & CAPRYLYL GLYCOL & PHENYLPROPANOL, PROPANEDIOL, BETAINE, PANTHENOL, SODIUM HYALURONATE, POLYSORBATE 20.

PETA Cruelty-Free and Vegan

6M   PET   V

Made in the UK.
Unit 20 Hewitt Bus Pk
Winstanley Rd
Wigan
WN5 7XB
UGLOWTAN.COM
info@uglowtan.com

5 060756 070073

uGlow®

Intelligent Tanning
For a Natural Glow

e 250ml / 8.45FL.OZ

As WordPress is open source, there's a wide selection of impressive themes and plugins. A theme is the style and design of the website, and a plugin is an add-on feature that extends the capabilities of the CMS.

The best themes I've come across have been from ThemeForest.com. The most useful plugins I've used include Elementor, which will allow you to build pages using a drag-and-drop interface, and Yoast SEO, which will give you capabilities to optimise your website for search engines, which is something we will discuss later in this book (page 192).

To use WordPress you will need hosting. Most hosting service providers now offer a single-click installation, meaning you don't need to get your head around MySQL databases like I did when I started my journey. Additionally, there is a wealth of training materials available to assist you in mastering WordPress. A simple Google search will present you with plenty of options.

WEBFLOW

The last platform I want to mention is Webflow, an application allowing you to design and build responsive websites in a browser-based visual editor. At the time of writing, I'm using this for my current website.

In my previous full-time design role, I designed websites but did not build them. As I didn't know how to code, I would design the site, then pass the designs to a web developer who would construct them using code, creating functional websites. The challenge I faced with this approach was that I lost control and was never entirely satisfied with the final product.

My lack of coding knowledge also meant that WordPress sometimes became a headache. Yes, I could find themes I liked and could build a decent website quickly without writing code, however, I often faced the problem that they looked good on a desktop device but not on mobile. Since a high percentage of my website traffic came from mobile devices, this was a problem.

I had the option to hire web developers to sort any problems – and that's one tangible benefit of an open-source platform – but I longed for a solution that gave me control of the design. That's when Webflow came on the scene.

Webflow allows me to design what I want in a browser-based visual editor with complete control at every breakpoint. I also particularly love that it enables me to build my own CMS pages with only the fields I need, unlike WordPress, which tends to be bloated with more options than I ever need. Thanks to the ability to design various CMS pages, I can now quickly and easily add to and edit my portfolio, podcast and blog.

The downside to Webflow is that there's a lot to learn, especially for someone completely new to web design. However, Webflow's free training courses are superb, to the point, and entertaining to watch as well.

Web design can be complicated, but don't forget you can hire a web designer to take the pain off your hands. If you have the money to invest, that's an option to consider. It will allow you to focus your time on logo design. If you're struggling to afford it, perhaps you can do a trade swap?

For further support, I have listed helpful website design tools and resources at the back of this book (page 313).

CREATE A BRAND IDENTITY

Don't worry too much about your logo and identity when you start out. The sooner your website is live, the sooner you can promote it. Simply typing your name in a nice font will be sufficient as a temporary logo to get the site up and running.

Since you're a logo designer, it only makes sense that you'll eventually have a great logo and supporting identity of your own. Designing a logo for yourself can be challenging, so treat it like a client project and give yourself a deadline. However, I know too well that when you're a designer, you'll probably want to change it. I've personally changed mine at least three times.

When I designed my first logo, I didn't know what I was doing, so I did something I thought looked cool. As I learned more and began to take the business more seriously, I redesigned the logo to have more of a professional feel to it.

I committed to that direction for a few years, but as my business and knowledge grew, I started to think of clever and exciting ideas, so I eventually came to a simple solution whereby the 'o' and the 'g' of Logo were linked to create a pair of glasses. It's a simple logo that works effectively for me and the Logo Geek brand, so it will probably remain this way forever.

Whatever you do, don't let it become an obstacle to progress. Create something, commit and move on.

Logo Geek 'Logo' design by Ian Paget

CASE STUDIES

Your online portfolio will become one of your most important asset as a designer. However, if you only show images, you're missing the opportunity to show off your expertise, process and thinking.

A lot of thought goes into a logo, so I recommend creating a case study for each design you include. This is a page of content that discusses the project, explains who the client is, the challenges faced and how you solved them.

To support that content, I create high-quality images of the logo in use and seek out the most suitable images relevant to the project. I'll also modify them in Photoshop so that the colours and styles are consistent across all the images. I've known designers who have taken real photos of the logo in use, which looks more impressive than a mockup. If you have that option, do it.

Whenever I've redesigned a logo, I showcase a before-and-after image. It helps illustrate the impact I've had on the business, which I believe appears more impressive than just displaying the new design alone.

Some designers include development work too, such as images of sketches. Personally, I prefer to create blog content for any behind-the-scenes work and keep case studies focused on the final solution.

The ultimate goal of a case study is to share the thought process so that those exploring the website can understand how you approach design. This will impress potential clients and give them confidence that you know your stuff.

MARKETING YOUR WEBSITE

Having a website has been crucial to my journey to becoming a full-time logo designer, however, simply having a website wasn't what attracted clients.

You can have the most stunning portfolio, but if people can't find it, it won't attract clients. For people to find your website, you need to promote it.

Marketing is another rabbit hole and there are many books and resources on the subject, however, in this book, I want to focus on the techniques that have worked effectively for me. This has ranged from quick wins that has produced effective results immediately, to longer-term strategies involving ongoing activities that will continue to reap rewards long term. Let's dive into each of these.

USE YOUR EXISTING NETWORK

With a website ready, you're now able to share it directly with friends, family and acquaintances in your existing network. This is how I got my very first design projects, so I recommending doing all you can to make sure everyone you know is aware you're designing logos. The more people that know what you do, the better.

I know hundreds of designers through design events and online communities, however, in day-to-day interactions, I've met very few. So it's likely that the average person has only met a couple of designers, if any. That means you could become the "one designer" that people know in your circle. So when they, their friends or colleagues are looking for a designer, who do you think they'll remember? That will be you.

SHARE YOUR WORK

Showing your work and what you're capable of doing is really important for attracting new work, so every time I finish a case study, I'll share it on social media.

I'll create a post with a summary of the project, along with some nice images and a link to the case study. Actively doing this has helped to remind everyone of my skillset, strengthening their confidence in my ability as a designer, so I recommend you do the same.

Your existing network will see the posts, however, and more importantly, a business owner outside your network may also stumble across the post, so if you include a link to your website too, they'll be able to see more examples, learn more about you, and they'll hopefully get in touch.

NETWORK TO BUILD RELATIONSHIPS

In the business world, there's an endless supply of networking events specifically designed to help business owners meet other business owners. They exist in person and online, and some even have talks or special events planned to make them worthwhile.

I vividly remember my first in-person networking event. I read how you should come equipped with business

cards and a short speech about what you do, known as an elevator pitch. I dressed smartly, arrived early, and I felt nervous and out of place from the moment I stepped in.

I've struggled with social anxiety most of my life, so I would awkwardly approach people who looked lost. We'd chat for a few minutes, exchange elevator pitches and swap business cards. After the event, I would follow up with a polite email, although in most cases, I have never seen or spoken to those people since.

I've now thrown that approach out of the window and taken a more honest direction that's more true to who I am. I now only attend the events that interest me as a business owner and I dress however I want. This means I have a genuine reason for attending beyond finding clients, have a common interest with those who attend, and, more importantly, feel more comfortable and confident.

I now treat any form of networking as making friends. It just happens to be with business owners. Then, should they ask me what I do, rather than using some fancy elevator pitch, I'll simply tell them that "I design logos." This approach is less scripted and more genuine, and the conversation takes shape from there.

I now have fun at networking events. Rather than just making connections for the sake of it, I've started to make genuine friendships. I want to actually keep in touch with the people I meet rather than pretend like I did after my first few events.

It's very likely that most people you meet won't ever need a logo designed, so there's no need to force your services down their throats.

Cambridge Centre for AI in Medicine logo design by Ian Paget

I like the advice given in the interview I did with Joana Galvão of Gif Design Studios, where she shares some great networking tips (listen @ logogeek.uk/5.6). Once she gets to know someone, she'll ask something along the lines of, "Do you know anyone who might be interested in getting a logo designed?" If they say no, she'll move on, however, the hope is that they or a business friend might need her services now or in the future.

By taking this approach, you're making people aware of what you do, so when the time is right, you'll hopefully be the first person that comes to mind, and you'll gain plenty of referrals.

REFERRALS & COLLABORATIONS

When your work is good, your clients will refer their friends and family to you if they need your services. Something you may not realise though, is that referrals can come from other designers too, which has happened to me. I've also referred projects to other designers too.

Imagine if you had so much work on that you couldn't schedule any more projects. Would you turn work away or would you prefer to provide support by passing the enquiry on to a talented designer friend? By doing that, you're helping out a friend and still serving your client.

Having an extra pair of trusted hands to complete a project can often be a lifesaver, so if you're good at what you do and open to projects, make sure your designer friends are aware. Ideally, you want to become that trusted go-to designer. To increase the odds of that happening, offer an incentive. When a project is sent your way, reward them with a percentage of the sale. That way, it's a win-win situation for you both.

Just remember that referrals can come from anyone. That's why building your network and reputation as a logo designer is so important, a topic we'll discuss later in the book (page 214).

SEARCH ENGINE OPTIMISATION (SEO)

Almost everyone who uses the internet will use search engines, the most popular being Google. Search for the thing you need and you'll be presented with a list of relevant results. The top results are usually paid ads and are marked as such, but the rest are organically determined by several sophisticated algorithms.

When a business owner is looking for a designer, if they don't already know someone, they will probably head to Google. They'll punch in a search term, such as "logo designer," and visit the websites of those listed on the first few pages. As my website ranks well on Google, this is how I currently get most of my clients. This is the result of understanding the power of Search Engine Optimisation (SEO). Getting high-ranking search results didn't happen overnight though. I've worked on my website continually for years, with intent.

SEO is a huge topic that's forever changing, so any advice written in a book is likely to become quickly dated. For that reason, at the back of this book, I have listed several valuable resources that I can recommend checking to keep up to date (page 311).

Although it's a forever-changing area, there are several factors that I believe won't change any time soon, so let's dive into each of these.

WELL-WRITTEN CONTENT

When you perform a search, Google's spiders will crawl the billions of websites available. In seconds, it will provide a list of websites that it deems the most relevant. Which is more likely to show in those top results? A page of images, or a well-written piece of engaging content? The answer is obvious.

You can't just share images of your design work to rank on Google. You will need to include unique well-written content too. The obvious opportunities to add content are on your main pages, such as your home page, your "about" page and case studies. You might also want to consider creating content that answers the frequently asked questions your target clients will be searching for. You could also go behind the scenes of projects and share your lessons and experiences. The possibilities are endless.

There are, however, a few things that Google doesn't like. For example, Google doesn't like "thin" content, so write at least 300 words per page. It also doesn't like duplicate content, so create your own content rather than copy from others. It also doesn't like people who game the system. Since the origins of Google, there have been numerous tricks and hacks to get that top position, but Google is continually creating more and more sophisticated algorithms that will reward those who do good and penalise those who try to game the system with black-hat techniques.

How to avoid being penalised? Focus on serving your audience. Write good-quality, well-structured, unique, and engaging content that's helpful, which is what I've been doing.

PINK NOISE

Pink Noise logo design by Ian Paget

KEYWORDS

Throughout your content, you want to include the words or phrases you want to rank for.

In the early days of the internet, you could do what was known as "keyword stuffing," where you'd repeat this word (or phrase) throughout your content to get quick results. Sadly, those days are long gone, and if you were to do that now, Google would determine it to be poor-quality content.

Google has become so sophisticated that it knows words that are associated. For example, if writing about logo design, the algorithms know that terms such as Adobe Illustrator, sketching and vector are associated. Although you shouldn't keyword stuff, you should include variants of your chosen keyword and related words. If you're writing quality content, you'll do this naturally, however, there's no harm in working to ensure your content performs well.

As an exercise, I write down the word or phrase I wish to target. I'll then list all the words that relate to it, including plural variants. Once my article is complete, I go through my content to include as many of these words as possible.

If you want to do this properly, I recommend performing what SEO experts call "keyword research." This will provide you with specific data that will help you to understand what people are searching for and how many are searching for it. The SEO resources shared at the back of this book will help you discover and learn more about this topic (page 311).

HEADER TAGS

Aside from writing high-quality content, you need to structure it properly with headings that break down the content to make it pleasant to read. However, don't just change the text size of headings. You'll need to use Header Tags (H1, H2, H3 etc) within the code so that Google knows the difference.

If you're web savvy, you can add Header Tags manually into the HTML, but thankfully most content editors allow you to control the headings, which will apply the relevant code.

A H1 tag is for the main title, which tells users (and Google) what your page is about. In the same way as a book only has one title, your page should only ever have a single H1. H2 tags are for the next level of sections, and then H3's, H4's, and H5's etc can be used to break the content down further.

The page heading (H1 tag) is one of the most critical parts of a page, so I recommend you make it clear and descriptive. If you answer a question, write the title as someone would ask it.

METADATA: TITLE & DESCRIPTIONS

When you search on Google, the results will show a list of titles, each with a short description below it. In most cases, what you see here is metadata. This is content hidden in the page's code to tell search engines what the page is about and that your content is relevant to the search term.

If you're using WordPress, adding a plugin such as Yoast SEO will give you control of this. Other platforms, including SquareSpace and Webflow, have this capability built-in.

At the time of writing this book, it's recommended to keep title tags to 55 characters or fewer, including spaces, and meta descriptions at 150 to 160 characters in length. These should also be unique for every page on your website.

SOCIAL METADATA

When you share a link on social media, you'll notice a preview, including an image, the page title, a summary of the content, and more. This is social metadata, sometimes referred to as Open Graph. Similar to adding metadata for titles and descriptions, you add this to control how the content is displayed when shared on social media.

IMAGES: FILE NAMES & ALT TAGS

When creating images for your website, give the file name a short description, and include the keyword or use a related term. So, for example, if your image is of a logo you designed for Stannard Construction and you've presented it nicely on a business card, I would name the file something like "stannard-construction-logo-business-card.jpg" rather than a random name like "image-5.jpg."

You'll also want to add image alt text, which means "alternative text." You use this to describe the image, allowing Google, a machine, to understand what the image is. More importantly, it benefits visually impaired users who use screen readers when browsing.

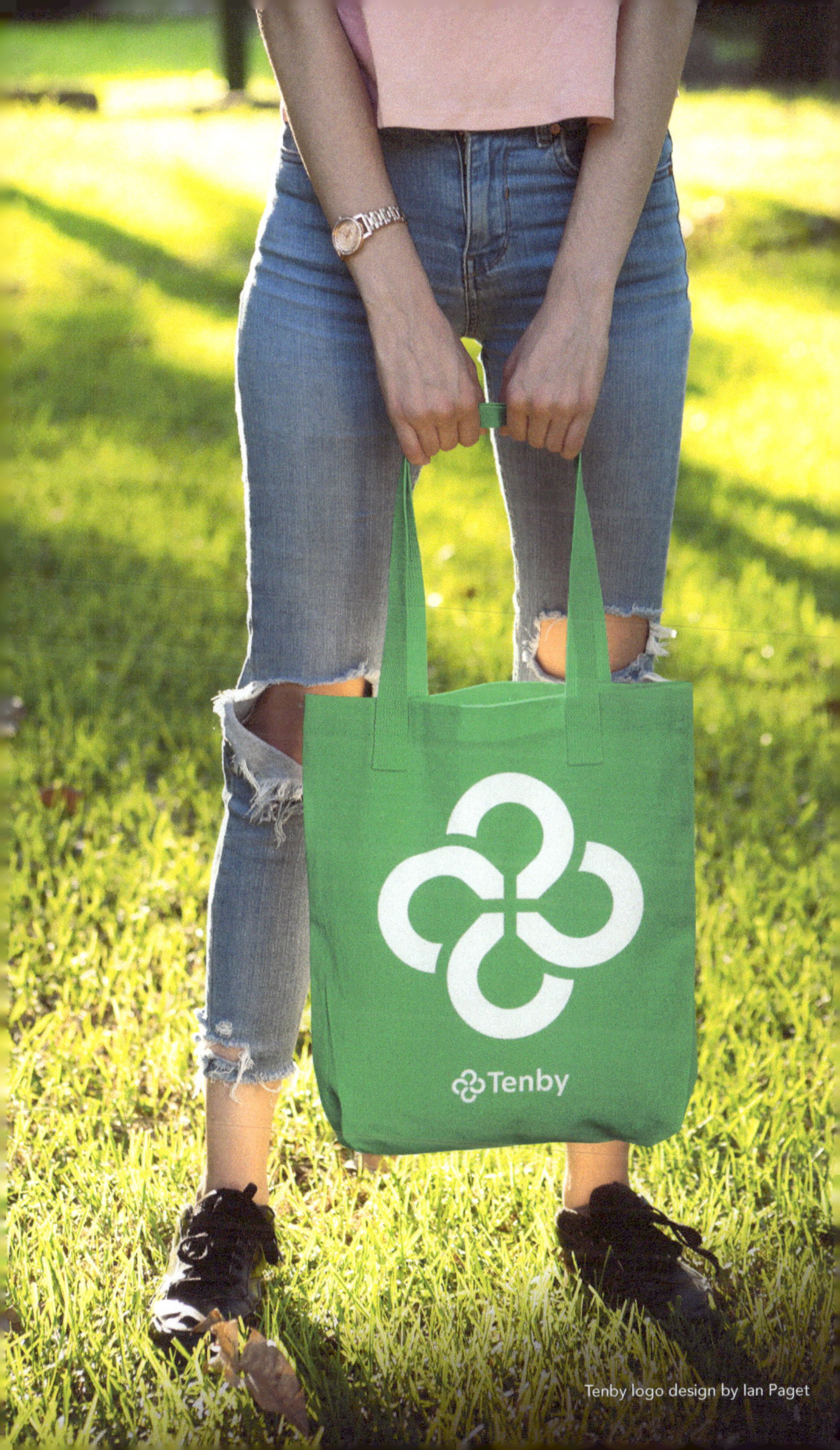

Tenby logo design by Ian Paget

LINKS TO INTERNAL & EXTERNAL CONTENT

When adding additional content to a website, it's natural to begin discussing topics that have been covered previously. In such cases, I recommend including a text link within the new content that directs visitors to the relevant page, allowing them to dig deeper into the topic. This is beneficial for readers, although it enhances the website's appeal to Google too.

It's important to link to external websites as well. Not including external links is like writing a research report without a bibliography. People will wonder where the information comes from. Sites with no outbound links are also dead ends, so Google could deem the website to be unhelpful.

Adding links to high-quality content creates a better, more rewarding experience for those who visit the website. This also helps Google verify the importance of a page or website, so the effort will be rewarded.

BACKLINKS

A backlink is a link from an external website that links back to yours. Whenever you receive a backlink, it's a bit like a positive vote. The more "votes" you can get, especially from sites with authority, the more it will positively impact your website's search visibility.

There was a time when companies would fabricate this, using link farms to give the illusion of thousands of links. However, this is now deemed a black-hat technique, so those who do this will get penalised by Google. Now Google looks at the quality of the links received rather than the quantity.

BRITISH™
OVERLAND

Land Rover Defender Hire

British Overland logo design by Ian Paget

As you create good content and build authority, you should naturally attract links back to your website, but you can also work to attract them. One promising approach is to write high-quality guest blog posts for other relevant websites. I want to stress the importance of relevance. Being a designer, ideally, those links should come from other sites about design or business or something else related to your target audience. The more relevant, the more it will help your SEO efforts.

You'll find that most blog owners will appreciate the contribution, especially if you write excellent content. It's a win-win situation for you both.

It can be a little more challenging to get featured on the more prominent industry websites, though. That's not to say it's impossible, but you may need to network with the authors who frequently contribute to find out the best way to get your content featured.

Some of the best links I've received have come from knowing content creators, so it's worth reaching out and getting to know a few. Occasionally, blog writers will create content with opinions and advice from a group of experts. If the writer knows you and knows of your skills and expertise, they'll probably ask you to contribute. In this instance, you need to be reactive. If you're ever asked, jump on that opportunity as a priority!

The more influential you become, the more likely you'll be featured, so continually building a reputation – which I discuss later in the book – will help increase the odds of attracting those more valuable, quality links (page 214).

PAGE SPEED

The speed of the website makes a big difference, not only to the user experience but to Google too. Countless things can impact page speed, from the website's hosting to the code, the images, and more.

When I first built my website, I used shared hosting, the cheaper option. As my business grew, I noticed my website was running incredibly slowly, which got worse at peak times. This is because when using shared hosting, the website is on the same server as multiple websites. As more people visit those other websites, it would slow down my website. To solve this, I invested in dedicated hosting. This costs more, but it drastically sped up my website, making it a better experience for visitors and ultimately improving my search results.

I also used Cloudflare, a content distribution network (CDN). You can picture a CDN as copies of your website on servers in multiple locations worldwide. It distributes the load of your content to give users faster and more reliable access to your site.

I continually worked hard to optimise the images and code on my website to ensure the pages load as fast as possible. The faster, the better. If your website's running slow, find out what could be slowing it down and fix it.

WEBSITE BUILD & SECURITY

The quality of the website build matters. Not only does good code allow the website to run quickly and be easy to use, it will also impact search results.

Ideally, the website will be responsive, allowing the site to operate effectively on all devices, from mobile to desktop. It should also be secure, using HTTPS with a supporting SSL certificate, which will protect your website from hackers stealing confidential information.

TARGET LOCAL

My website performs very well on Google. When I first built it, I never imagined it would rank on Google for generic terms such as "logo design." But it eventually did.

I've always felt confident that I could rank on Google for local search terms, such as "logo design in Manchester," which are much less competitive. With some effort and time, I managed to secure that top spot, attracting numerous enquiries from local business owners. (Note that, at the time of writing, I have just relocated to Birmingham, which is a slightly more competitive area, so I'm still working to reach position number one for Logo Design Birmingham, however, I did manage to rank on page one fairly quickly).

Although there's no guarantee the same will work for you, here's an overview of the steps I took to achieve this:

- I mention my location on the homepage in the H1 title, content and metadata.

- I added my business address and telephone number to the footer of my website and the contact page.

- I added my business to as many online directories as possible, using the same address and telephone number as on my website.

Stannard Construction logo design by Ian Paget

- I added my details to Google My Business.

- I included my address and telephone details in schema markup, which is code that helps Google better understand the website's information.

Your address and telephone number are two of the most important components of this and should be in the same consistent format everywhere you submit your details. However, if you're working from home or renting a property, your address might not be something you can share.

To get around this, I use a virtual address. Numerous companies provide offices and co-working spaces for small businesses and entrepreneurs. This is an ideal way to have a dedicated location to grow and run your business – somewhere you can meet clients face-to-face in a professional environment. They usually have a friendly receptionist, can take calls for you, and will accept and pass on your post. Many of these locations also offer a virtual office, meaning you can give the impression you operate from this location. It's been worth it for me, even with the fees involved, as it gives me an address at a respectable location in my local city centre.

FURTHER LEARNING

This is only a tiny sample of the things that will help improve your chances of ranking on Google, although if you focus on these, you'll substantially increase your odds of being found. Google uses hundreds of factors, which change over time as algorithms evolve. Refer to the SEO and Marketing resources at the back of this book to expand on the information provided here (page 310).

PAID ADVERTISING

There are many forms of paid advertising from print to web. However, the advice shared here is geared towards online advertising.

As my organic SEO results have been a success to date, paid advertising isn't an option I've used much myself, however, I have picked up some good advice from Mash Bonigala, the founder and CEO of SpellBrand, which I feel worth sharing.

SpellBrand has had great success using Facebook advertising, which allows companies to target specific audiences. It works well for them as a branding agency because they don't promote identity design to everyone. Instead, they create a tailored landing page for each industry they wish to target. This means they can target one key demographic at a time and create messaging, imagery and a portfolio that resonates with them. As it speaks directly to that audience and shows relevant examples to their industry, the conversion rate is significantly higher than that of a generic ad and landing page.

There's much more to learn about paid advertising than I have shared here, however, this example demonstrates that if you intend to pay for advertising, you should prepare carefully to get the biggest bang for your buck.

STANDING OUT FROM THE CROWD

I don't know the exact figure, but I'm going to guess that there are millions of designers out there, so if you want to make a living as a logo designer, you'll want to find every possible way to stand out. One way to do that is to "niche down" by focusing on serving a specific target audience or offering a distinct style.

Logo design as a skillset is a niche. You can become known as an excellent generalist logo designer who serves every business. That's what I've done for the most part. But niching down further certainly has its competitive advantages, so if I was starting from scratch knowing what I do now, I would niche down.

I'm well aware that choosing an area to focus on can be difficult, so at first, you may wish to work with all types of businesses, and that's okay. But over time, you might find you prefer working with certain business sectors. Now that I've been designing logos seriously for several years, I'm seeing more and more science and medical companies approach me, and since they contribute to the world's greater good, I'm drawn to these projects too. Eventually, as I've done so much in this area, I plan to create a new brand focused on this market.

I could happily continue working with all industries, and it's okay if you want to do that. But there are some incredible advantages to niching down which I want to share so you can weigh up your options.

Optevo

Email

Password

LOGIN

Forgot Email Address or Password?

Don't have an account? Sign up here.

RELEVANT PORTFOLIO

If you're a good designer, you can probably design a strong solution for any industry. However, some customers will like to see that you understand their industry and will want to see previous examples. If you can't show anything or lack knowledge of their market sector, that can sometimes be off-putting.

When you niche down, you can have a portfolio and supporting case studies full of work relevant to that industry. When a potential client from that sector lands on your portfolio, they see you deeply understand their industry, and they'll immediately trust that you can help.

Remember, you attract the type of work you show. If you don't have any relevant portfolio pieces, create some, even if they're fictional.

PERSONALISED HEADINGS & CONTENT

There's a saying in the business world that "when you target everyone, you reach no one." Sure, there are business owners out there who need a logo designer, so a generic welcome message will do the job (it works for me), however, if you make your headline and content more personalised, it will increase the volume of enquiries you receive.

Consider, for example, as a generalist designer, you might have a heading such as "I help business owners design logos," but if you were to target restaurants, you might tailor your messaging to be "I help restaurant owners attract more customers with logo design." If you were a restaurant owner, which would you choose? It should be an obvious choice.

This extends far beyond a simple heading. It runs through every piece of content you work on, allowing you to create clear, actionable advice targeted at the industry you wish to attract. For example, suppose you start a blog or podcast as a generalist. In that case, you'll probably share design advice that's more likely to attract other designers. Then imagine you're targeting restaurants. You could create relevant, helpful information such as "Restaurant Branding Tips" or a study of the 10 best-designed restaurants in your area.

In this scenario, I'd consider creating a podcast all about restaurants where I interview restaurant owners. This wouldn't be a design podcast. It would target restaurant owners and break down all the topics that could help them succeed. All the knowledge and advice would come from the guests, and I'd act as a curious outsider pulling all the fantastic advice together. This would allow me to network directly with some of the industry's biggest names while also becoming known to anyone interested in the content.

Creating content in this way demonstrates that you have an understanding of your chosen sector, and enables you to grow a deeper understanding of the industry.

PERFORM BETTER ON GOOGLE

Another key benefit of targeted content is that you'll start to rank high on Google for search terms relevant to your chosen industry, allowing you to get much faster organic results. It's taken me years to rank well for generic industry terms that are highly competitive, but when targeting a niche, you have much less competition, so it's easier and faster to rank on page one of Google for search terms associated with that industry.

BECOME KNOWN AS THE EXPERT

As you create and share case studies, you'll become known for your work in that industry. This means you're much more likely to receive referrals than a generalist.

A designer friend, Craig Burton, runs a business called School Branding Matters in New Zealand. Whenever I receive an enquiry from a school, I think of him – so much so that I consider passing school-related leads on to him, as I know he has a deeper understanding of the sector than I ever will.

EASIER TO ASK FOR REFERRALS

Niching down makes it easier to ask for referrals too. For example, suppose you've recently finished working on a project for a restaurant. In that case, it's pretty easy to ask, "Do you know any other restaurant owners who need help with their business identity?"

CREATE A RELEVANT PRODUCT OFFERING

Consider creating a product offering tailored to that sector. For example, if you design logos for estate agents, you may wish to offer a package where you design a logo, a "for sale" sign and a property information leaflet. You can even create templates and processes to speed up the delivery of these items to generate greater profits.

FORMULA FILM

Formula Film logo design by Ian Paget

EASIER TO NETWORK

Networking becomes much easier, as you know exactly who you must speak to. You can attend events and join online communities specifically designed for the industry you wish to target. Remember not to be a slimy salesperson… just make friends with the right people.

YOU BRING GREATER VALUE

When you specialise, over time, you will gain valuable insight into that industry. Potential clients will see value in that knowledge, and that gives them an increased sense of trust in you. With increased confidence and fewer competitors, you can command higher prices.

YOU CAN STILL SAY YES TO OTHER WORK

The belief that you can't take on any other work can put people off niching down. But that's not true. The key is to focus your marketing and networking efforts on targeting and attracting a specific audience, then, once you get an enquiry, it's yours for the taking, whatever industry the prospect falls under.

Another concern may be that the work becomes repetitive. However, you can't know this until you try. Don't forget you can always pivot, so if you try something that doesn't feel right or doesn't work, try something else.

PART 11

BUILDING REPUTA-TION

IF YOU WANT TO DESIGN LOGOS FOR A LIVING, YOU'LL NEED TO BECOME KNOWN AS THE GO-TO PERSON FOR LOGO DESIGN SERVICES. THAT REQUIRES YOU TO BUILD A REPUTATION.

IN THIS SECTION, I SHARE THE ACTIVITIES I CONTINUALLY PERFORM TO BUILD MY PERSONAL BRAND.

Building a reputation as a logo designer is something I've worked hard on, so in this section, I share the methods I've used to position myself as an expert on logo design. This includes social posting, writing, podcasting, video content, awards and juries, and social proof.

SOCIAL POSTING

There's a long list of social platforms, each governed by its own set of rules, but the key to success with any platform is consistency. There are only so many hours in the day, so showing up on every platform frequently isn't feasible for most.

My approach is to pick one and do it well. That way, I've been able to dedicate my time to learning everything there is to know about that one platform. Plus, I have the time and energy to post good content and show up consistently.

Think of a social platform as a fire. You will fail if you try to light ten fires at once. Although, if you dedicate all your time and energy to one, you'll have a strong and steady fire burning. With this approach, once you do have a fire burning, all you need to do to keep it lit is throw fuel on it now and again, and that's the same for social media.

Once you have built a thriving community of dedicated followers on one platform, you can step away to create success on a second platform. You'll only need to check back on the previous one to keep the momentum going.

Early in my journey, I put considerable energy into building a following on Twitter, now known as X, which at the time was one of the most popular social platforms.

As it's a micro-blogging platform, allowing only a limited number of characters at that time, it was a convenient platform to fit around a day job. I could post when it was convenient for me, be it when eating breakfast, when waiting for a train, or… and being entirely honest… when sitting on the toilet…

BUT WHAT DO YOU POST?

You can continually create your own content, but you don't need to. I've kept a list of good blogs and resources around logo design, and when it comes to posting, I will share that content along side my own. Although it's not my content, I'll become known for continually sharing interesting and valuable information and news about my area of expertise, even if I didn't create that content.

There's plenty of useful tools out there to help you schedule your posting activity, which I'll list at the back of this book (page 312).

You will, however, need more than just posting to grow a quality audience. It's vital that you engage with others too. If someone messages you, make sure to reply. Start discussions and get involved in those started by others. The more people you interact with, the more engaged your network will become. You will slowly establish a reputation for providing value.

Whatever your chosen platform, be sure to study and understand the ins and outs of the platform to make the most of it.

WRITING

Writing is one of the best ways to share your knowledge and demonstrate that you know what you're talking about. However, if writing isn't your strength, you might feel that you're not up to the task. That's how I felt when I started, so I want to encourage you to try. I struggled with my writing in school, so I needed extra support. Then once I finished school, I did very little reading or writing as it wasn't something I enjoyed.

When I started working at a web design agency, as it was a small company, we were encouraged to write blog posts. Because I had to write daily, my writing skills started to improve. When I started my logo design business, I continued that trend of actively writing. As I was writing about a topic that interested me, I enjoyed it! Over the past ten years, my writing abilities have improved so much that I'm able to write this very book.

I used my blog initially as a way to document and share the lessons I was learning. Over time, I also used it to answer questions, go behind the scenes of my design process and share my journey as a designer.

Contributing guest posts to other popular design or business websites also enhances your reputation.

As you consistently write and share your knowledge, you'll become recognised for your writing and build a reputation in the process.

HOST A PODCAST

Podcasting is another form of content creation, where instead of writing what you know, you're speaking about what you know. Unlike blogging, where it's easy to hide behind your writing, podcasting allows people to hear your voice, enabling them to get to know, like, and trust you in the process.

A podcast can be a solo show, or you can co-host with others. You can also invite guests to provide more depth and perspective to your show.

I began *The Logo Geek Podcast* in 2017, although I didn't initially intend to build a reputation through it. The primary reason for starting this podcast was to boost my confidence, and growing my reputation turned out to be an incredible by-product of those efforts.

I've had problems with anxiety since I was young and have struggled with public speaking, even in small groups. In school, I did what I could to avoid these situations, and as I got older, it grew into a severe problem that held me back professionally. I sought help and was offered a form of talking therapy called Cognitive Behavioural Therapy (CBT), which helps manage problems by changing how you think and behave. In short, it requires you to confront your fears.

Podcasting became my entry point. When I pressed that record button, it brought up all the fears and anxieties I faced in any public situation. Here, I could confront them in a safe environment and control how far I pushed myself.

Lo-Fi Flow logo design by Ian Paget

At first, I did a few solo episodes, which are sadly no longer available. A few years later, I was a co-host on a friend's show, SideGig. Then I decided to throw myself in at the deep end and start a show of my own – And so *The Logo Geek Podcast* was born.

While I made many mistakes and fumbled over my words, the beauty of audio is that I can cut out what I don't like and re-record myself as many times as needed. As long as the final thing sounds good, that's all that matters, and as I do more, I get better. It took a few years, but I now feel confident as a podcast host and enjoy it. My show has been successful and has brought me many personal benefits, including helping to build a reputation.

If you plan to start your own podcast, in order to make the most of your show and set it apart from the rest, I recommend creating content that specifically caters to your chosen audience, rather than a show for designers, as I described earlier in the book (page 209). Podcasting is a fantastic networking tool, so it can open the door to business owners you couldn't approach any other way, and once they know, like, and trust you, they may eventually become a client.

Podcasts can be released in seasons, made up of as many episodes as you wish, or you can release an episode on a consistent date, such as weekly or monthly. My podcast started as seasons made up of ten episodes, and over time it has become a weekly show thanks to the support of sponsors, who help to fund the production of the show, enabling me to dedicate time to creating valuable content.

BE INTERVIEWED

There are thousands of podcasts out there covering just about every interest you can think of. Many also feature guests and are actively looking for interesting people to be on their show.

I've made it a personal mission to get on as many shows as possible, no matter the topic. The main reason for this has been to support the goal of building up my confidence, however, it has also allowed me to speak directly to new audiences who could potentially become followers or even clients. Most podcast hosts will create show notes for each episode, and on this page, they'll also include links to my website and social media channels. So even if nobody listens, I at least get a backlink, which contributes to my ongoing SEO and marketing efforts.

If, like me, you're not a confident speaker, being a guest on other podcasts can be a way to gradually build up the confidence to start a show of your own. If the opportunity comes up, go for it.

VIDEO CONTENT

Written content needs to be read carefully for the information to be absorbed. Audio content requires the audience to focus too, but ideal for situations where they're on the move and can't do much else, such as driving or walking.

With video, users can just sit back, watch and enjoy. Since you can make it captivating, showing imagery and audio, people are much more likely to focus entirely on the content. Video platforms like YouTube are also search engines, so if you create helpful content, people will search, find and consume it.

There are countless ways to share and watch video content. Almost every social channel allows you to share videos in some form, so there are ample opportunities to show your face and provide value.

If you dare to get on camera, it's an opportunity for people to get to know you, like you, and trust you. The perfect way to build a reputation. But if you're an introvert like me, video can be scary. At the time of writing this book, I still find getting on camera daunting and don't feel comfortable, so I haven't yet leveraged its full potential. That's not to say I don't try. I've pushed myself to do the occasional Instagram live. I've also been a guest on a few video podcasts. In general, if I'm invited to contribute to something that requires me to be on camera, I'll do it.

I see the immense value in video content, and will continue to throw myself into situations outside my comfort zone. I encourage you to do the same.

AWARDS & JURIES

You can forever brand yourself as an award-winning designer with just one award under your belt. Winning one not only boosts your confidence but also adds an impressive touch to your portfolio, helping to solidify your reputation as a designer.

Northumberland 250 logo design by Ian Paget

In the back of this book, I've compiled a list of several credible industry awards you might consider entering (page 302). Personally, I've had the privilege of securing a gold award at the International Visual Identity Awards and having my work featured multiple times in the Logo Lounge books. While it might not compare to the achievements of some of my designer friends, it's never been my focus.

Winning awards brings a multitude of benefits and can unlock exciting new opportunities. However, it's worth exercising caution, especially with some of the more expensive options out there. If you believe it's worth the investment, go for it.

Many of us work in isolation, and it's natural to seek validation that our designs are among the best. However, it's essential to recognise that awards are also businesses, and some may prioritise profits over recognition. That's why I've chosen a different path – to be on the jury instead. Serving on award juries carries just as much prestige as winning, and it positions me as an industry leader. Sometimes, I receive invitations, and in other cases, I volunteer.

In most cases, I have been selected for juries because I have built a substantial following on social media. In return, most agreements require me to write or post about the awards, which provides them with free publicity. I get value from it too, so it's a mutually beneficial arrangement.

QUALIFICATIONS & CERTIFICATIONS

If you have a degree or certification, mention it throughout your website. This will help demonstrate your knowledge and provide an additional layer of trust.

I don't personally have a formal design education. I do, however, have plenty of experience working within design teams, which can provide just as much trust. In my content, I'll mention my prior experience and name-drop the well-known companies I've designed for while in these positions.

Despite not having a degree, I actively work to earn certifications in areas relevant to logo design and branding, which I mention on my website and in sales proposals.

SOCIAL PROOF

If you're buying a new computer, how do you decide which is the best? Most of us will read the reviews, or you may ask a friend. Ultimately, the actions and attitudes of the people around you will influence your decision. This is known as social proof, and we can leverage this as designers.

Imagine if a client was choosing between two designers with equally strong portfolios. One only displays a portfolio. The other also mentions that they've won awards, been featured in reputable publications and have hundreds of reviews and social followers. Who would you choose? Who would you trust? Who will provide more value?

There may be no difference between the quality of service and the knowledge of the two designers, but there's immediately perceived trust gained from social proof. That's why I've made it an intentional part of my strategy.

We've already discussed many things that will impact social proof, for example, growing a large social following, winning awards, being on juries, being a podcast guest and gaining certifications. But there's more… You could get mentioned or featured in books and magazines or in articles on high-profile websites such as Forbes and Entrepreneur.

An easy way to get featured in a logo book is to join Logo Lounge. Every year they select the best from the designs uploaded and include them in a book. I've been fortunate that my work has been featured in a few and I've been on the jury too.

I've also been lucky enough to be featured in a few magazines, which has come from actively posting on Twitter/X. By posting and engaging on social media, your following will grow, and people in your industry will be drawn toward you. So when writers need an expert to contribute to a feature, they'll probably reach out to you because you're easy to find. This is how I got featured in Dot Net, Photoshop Creative, and 99U, and contributed articles to Creative Bloq. I've also been lucky enough to have been mentioned in Forbes, Entrepreneur, and AdWeek.

Pill Connect

A Smart Pill Dispenser

Easily track and record each pill dispense request made by participants and ensure that every single pill is accounted for.

www.pillconnect.com

09:30am
Dose dispensed 2 pills

The AdWeek mention was thanks to a guest I interviewed on my podcast. They needed opinions on several logos, and as I was one of the people in his network with knowledge of logo design, I was invited to contribute.

The Forbes and Entrepreneur features were thanks to a fellow freelance writer that contributes to a lot of prominent websites. As he often needs tips and opinions for his articles, I've become part of his trusted network of experts. This is why networking is so powerful!

In the end, your reputation will establish trust, and this trust will have a direct impact on the quality of leads you attract, the conversion rate of those leads, and the prices you can ask for. This is why I consistently strive to build my reputation, and why you should do the same.

WHY I'VE TARGETED DESIGNERS

Aside from case studies, most of my recurring content has been created to help other designers. At first, this was because my logo design business was a hobby and I used my blog and social channels to document my lessons.

As I've progressed in my journey, I've attended numerous business conferences and read lots of business books and I've learned that the "correct" approach would have been to define a target audience and create content that attracts them. In hindsight, this sounds obvious!

If I had this knowledge at the start of my journey, I might have approached everything differently, but having seen the results of my "errors," I've continued to intentionally target designers. There are a few reasons for this, however, most are related to Google search, which accounts for a large volume of my inbound leads.

By actively sharing design-related content in the form of blogs and podcasts, I'm building a following and a reputation for myself. My peers now see me as an expert on logo design, with some even calling me an "influencer." This has opened doors within the industry through interviews, guest blogging and judging opportunities, all of which attract relevant, authoritative links back to my website.

The average client is unlikely to search for or read any logo design–related content until they need a logo designer. As I'm actively creating a library of content about logo design, my website will hopefully continue to perform well on Google. This means that clients can find me when they need a logo designed.

If a prospective client finds my content, although a lot of the content won't be relevant to them, it's still enough to demonstrate that I have good knowledge of and passion for design. If they need a logo designer, they've found someone who can help, so they'll get in touch, and that's the goal.

Sharing design-related content equates to enquiries, and documenting and sharing what I've learned is beneficial for my education too. When I worked in a director position, I taught younger designers who joined the team. This opened my eyes to how much you improve from the moment you start to teach. Having to explain how and why you do something pushes you to a whole new level, so explaining the lessons I have learned enables me to become a better, more knowledgeable designer.

There's also the feeling that I am giving back to the next generation of designers. Although I have no formal education, I've spent years learning from books and through conversations with experienced designers, as well as from my own hands-on experience. It's only right to pass this knowledge on to others. I know all too well that if it wasn't for the generosity of the designers of previous generations who have documented their lessons, I wouldn't be where I am now, and I want to continue that trend. I hope you will too.

I've also built extra passive income streams from my content. For example, my podcast receives sponsorship. This is usually a nice up-front payment, so I'm getting paid to speak about a topic I love with people I admire. I also generate income through the products I endorse. This is known as affiliate marketing, where I'm provided with a unique link, and earn a commission when someone purchases the product using that link. This means that as I continue to learn, build a reputation, grow a following, and assist others, I also generate additional income. It's a win-win situation for everyone involved.

Making money from my content was never the goal, however, it's become a successful by-product of having a passion for a topic, and building a community around it. If you want to learn more about monetising your content, I recommend checking out *Smart Passive Income*, which is a blog, podcast and YouTube channel by Pat Flynn, who has taught me so much and been an inspiring figure throughout my journey.

Rule Zero logo design by Ian Paget

PART 12

SELLING LOGOS

ONCE YOU'VE BUILT A DECENT PORTFOLIO & STARTED TO ESTABLISH A REPUTATION AS A LOGO DESIGNER, YOU WILL INEVITABLY RECEIVE ENQUIRIES.

IN THIS SECTION, I'LL SHARE HOW I RESPOND TO ENQUIRIES, HOW I'VE WORKED OUT WHAT TO CHARGE & HOW I PREPARE PROPOSAL DOCUMENTS, CONTRACTS & INVOICES.

RESPONDING TO ENQUIRIES

When I started Logo Geek, I was fitting everything around a full-time job with a fairly long commute. The only time I could work on my business was late evenings and weekends. Taking telephone calls during the day was not feasible.

Because I had limited time, if I received an email, I would respond with a fairly long template reply that provided an overview of my process, a price and an estimated delivery time. This allowed me to quickly copy and paste the response, then make a few tweaks to the start of the email so that it felt personalised. Although somewhat impersonal and less effective than a telephone call, it worked more frequently than I expected and since I could only take on a couple of projects at a time, it was more than enough to keep me busy.

As I've progressed to focus on my logo design business full-time, my approach to sales has changed considerably. When starting my journey, as I had a day job, money wasn't an issue, so if my impersonal approach put people off, it didn't matter. However, once I was designing logos full time, I needed to make money, so every enquiry was an opportunity I didn't want to lose.

When someone gets in touch, they have probably also contacted a handful of other designers. Some people are looking for the cheapest option, but most are looking for the best they can afford. This means that every interaction is an opportunity to demonstrate my knowledge and instil confidence that I'm the right person for the job. Now, when I receive an enquiry by email, I respond with a short personalised email where I share my excitement for the project and ask if they're available for a call to discuss it further.

SPEAKING TO THE CLIENT

I pick up my phone, dial the number, and once they answer, in a positive voice, I'll say, "Hello, [insert customer name]. I'm following up on our email conversation. Is now still a good time to speak?" If it is, I will then ask a simple question: "Although you've provided an introduction in your original enquiry, as this is the first time we've properly spoken, do you want to talk through how I can help?"

This allows them to talk through where they are with their business and where they need help, and it makes them feel heard too. I'll listen carefully and take notes. Once they've shared their story, I discuss my process and how I can help solve their problem. I'll then ask if they have any follow-up questions or want me to expand on anything.

At this point, they'll usually ask, "How much does it cost?" This is when I provide a price, which I'll share how I work out shortly. Following that, I explain my payment structure, which involves receiving 50% upfront to schedule the project in, with the remaining 50% invoiced once the design has been approved.

I'll then pause and wait for their response. Be confident. Don't feel the need to suddenly reduce your cost. Just wait.

At this point, the discussion can go a few ways. The ideal scenario is that they want to proceed and will ask what the next steps are to get the ball rolling. Other times, they might be very interested and ask more questions to help with their decision-making. Quite frequently, though, they want time to think, or they need to discuss the project with a business partner, team or manager. In these cases, I will send over a proposal document, which I discuss in more detail later in the book (page 242).

Other times the price is out of their budget and that's okay. For research purposes, I ask what budget they had in mind. If it's a reasonable figure and I find the project of interest, I might negotiate, however, in most cases, I will help by pointing them in the right direction and wishing them all the best with the project.

Being friendly and helpful has always worked in my favour. There have been several occasions when the price was way out of their budget, but they appreciated the friendly help and support, and I gained their trust to the point that they pulled together the budget and returned to kick the project off! So never be rude or disrespectful to anyone.

I've often heard that you should discuss the budget as early as possible in the conversation to avoid wasting your time (or theirs). But first, I like to dedicate fifteen minutes to listening to their plans and talking through my process. This is so they understand how I'm different from the cheaper options on the market before hearing my price.

HOW MUCH DO I CHARGE?

When you first start designing logos, as you're still learning and don't have much experience, you're unlikely to get paid much. We all need to start somewhere though.

Look at every opportunity as an investment in your future. Opportunities are more valuable than money initially, so be thankful if you can get even a few. You can then gradually increase your prices as you improve. Only when you have a strong body of work and can demonstrate that you're the best person for the job will you get paid what you truly deserve. But how much should you charge once you do have the experience?

If you look at the market for logo design, the prices vary considerably. They start as low as a few dollars and go up into the millions. However, knowing exactly how much YOU should charge is not a simple question. Everyone's process, experience and location will differ considerably, affecting the price.

There's no single right way to do this. For example, you might choose to work on a handful of projects at a high price. Or you might churn out several a week at a lower price. How you position yourself in the market is up to you.

There are also different ways to price things. I've met designers who charge a fixed price for every project and I've met those who work out an individual price for each client based on the value to the company.

ATLAS

AUTOMATED
HIGH-THROUGHPUT
PLATFORM SUITE

There are many ways to do this. I don't have all the answers, and certainly not an expert on pricing, although I can share how I do it and what works for me.

I've positioned myself in the mid-range market and aim to take on up to two projects per week, which allows me to live comfortably. Since the average time I spend on a project remains relatively consistent, I've simplified things for myself by implementing a fixed pricing structure.

I will, however, quote a higher price for larger companies where I know there will be more decision-makers involved and where I want to invest more time, or if it's a simple project or one that I really want, if needed, I'll reduce my price.

Supply and demand will affect my prices too. I'll quote higher if I'm super busy, as I have nothing to lose and want to reduce the demand. If I'm a bit quiet, I might lower my price to close a sale if it's needed. There's nothing wrong with lowing your price if you remain profitable.

So let me explain how I work out that fixed cost.

I start by working out a base price. This is the minimum I can charge in order to earn enough to cover my living costs. By working this out, I can always charge higher but also reduce my price where needed. As long as it's no lower than my base price, I can be comfortable knowing that I can still afford to live.

This base price is based on the average length of time I spend on a project. While I don't charge by the hour, knowing how long I usually spend on a project means I can work out a suitable average project price.

Once I know the average time I spend on a project, I can multiply that by my hourly rate. I'm sure you're now wondering how I work out my hourly rate, so let's discuss.

WORKING OUT MY HOURLY RATE

I start by determining how much I want to earn in a year. This can be as high as you want – just be realistic.

It's helpful to determine your living costs, including your mortgage or rent, bills, travel, food, entertainment, and so on. You'll want to earn a little more to save up too, but knowing how much life costs will give you an idea of how much you need to make each month to live comfortably. For example, let's say this is £100k per year. (A nice round number!)

Whatever figure you've worked out, divide that by 10 to give yourself a monthly goal. I divide by 10 because I'm subtracting a month for time off and a month for non-billable tasks such as networking, marketing, calls, emails and other administrative tasks. So, for example, £100k divided by 10 is £10k.

Next, I determine how many hours I can realistically work per week. Typically this is 40 hours (8 hours a day, 5 days a week). I then multiply this by 4 to work out roughly how many hours I'll be working each month. So 40 hours multiplied by 4 means I'll be working in the neighbourhood of 160 hours per month.

To get my hourly rate, I divide my monthly goal by how many hours I'll work each month. So if my monthly goal is £10k and I divide that by 160 hours, my hourly rate works out at £62.50.

WORKING OUT MY BASE PROJECT COST

To determine my base price, I work out how long a project usually takes, including any revisions. I then multiply that by my hourly rate.

If I spend around 3 days on a project (8 hours a day), the time I spend per project is 24 hours. So 24 multiplied by £62.50 equals £1,500. So if I want to earn an annual salary of £100k, the minimum I need to charge per project is £1,500.

Now I know a base price, I can work out a fixed project cost. I want to make a profit, so in this example, I'll increase this a little to around £1,800.

So it's clear, this is not what I charge, but I hope it will help you determine what YOU should charge based on your circumstances.

CHARGE PER PROJECT, NOT PER HOUR

This approach is only a starting point. As you get more experienced, you'll inevitably work faster. So the idea of working out a price based on your hourly rate will eventually make no sense. By that logic, the more efficient you become, the lower your prices will be.

As you gain more experience, it's advisable to raise your prices. This is where having a project price comes in handy. It's a fixed amount that you can consistently raise, regardless of the actual time spent on the project. There's no ceiling to what you charge as long as you can find clients who will pay those prices.

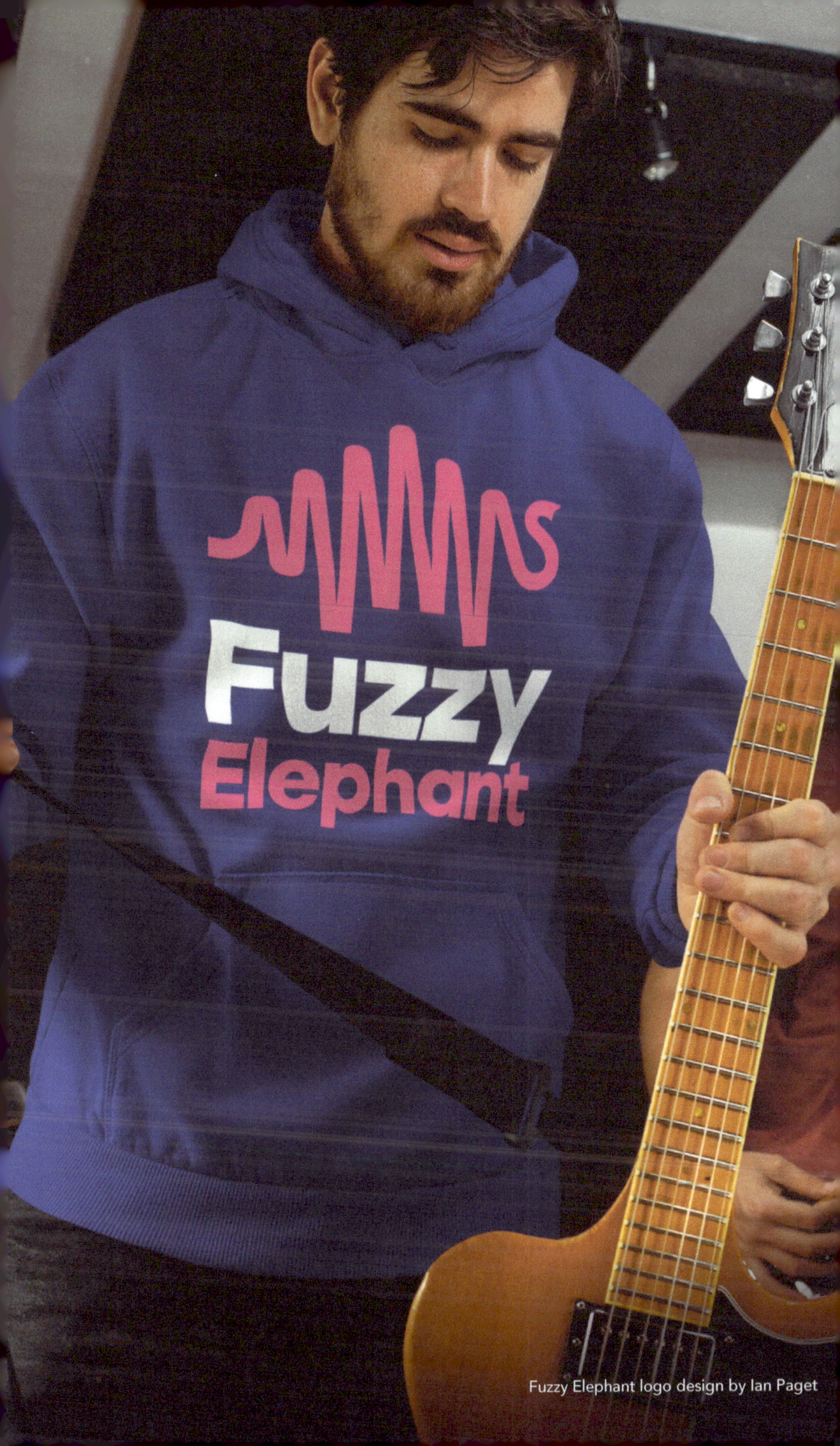

Fuzzy Elephant logo design by Ian Paget

UNDERSTAND YOUR POSITION IN THE MARKET

Once you've established a reputation, hopefully, you'll attract clients who will only want to work with you. In that case, you can name your price. However, until you reach that stage, you're one of many.

Clients will shop around, so it's helpful to understand what the market looks like. Not so you can be the cheapest, but so you know how you compare with others in the industry, particularly at the price point you wish to target. The market changes frequently, so I can't give you the answers here. Discover what's out there on your own, as if you were a client. That information will become invaluable.

PROPOSAL DOCUMENT

You had a great call, but your prospect now needs to decide which provider is the best fit. In most cases, they will want to discuss the options with a business partner or the management team. You can cross your fingers and hope for the best, or increase your odds by sending an impressive Proposal Document that allows you to stand out from the rest.

In the beginning, I didn't have a Proposal Document. I wrote everything in an email, and if the prospect decided to proceed, I put together a contract and invoice to kick things off. However, after going full-time, I found sending a Proposal Document to be a superb way to impress the client and demonstrate how I differ from the cheaper options. It makes me look more professional and trustworthy than my competitors, allowing me to convert more projects at a higher price point.

WHAT'S INSIDE A PROPOSAL DOCUMENT?

There's no set way of making a proposal, but I like to include the following:

- A brief introduction about me and my experience.

- An overview of my design process.

- An overview of how I can help.

- A price with an estimate of timescales.

- A summary of the final deliverables.

- A few testimonials.

- A few relevant examples from my portfolio.

- My contact details.

Note that this doesn't include the terms and conditions or any formalities; those are covered in a contract, which I will send at a later date if they decide to move forward. This document is intended to impress and show that I'm the most suitable candidate for the job.

To speed up this process, I've created a template in InDesign that I can quickly customise. I recommend you do the same. Unfortunately, you're not guaranteed to secure every project that comes your way, so the faster you can create a proposal while giving a sense of quality, the better.

CONTRACTS

Once I have confirmation that a prospect wants to proceed with a project, I prepare a formal Contract detailing the project scope and the terms and conditions of the agreement.

As a starting point, I used a contract template I found online. You'll find links to a few great examples at the back of this book (page 315). But any contract template should be just that – a starting point. You'll need to modify and adjust it to fit your requirements.

This usually includes the following:

• The project scope.

• A list of the final deliverables.

• Payment structure.

• Payment details.

• Ownership and rights.

• Details about amendments and feedback.

• Cancellation and project suspension.

An important lesson I've learned is to never blame your client when facing a problem. Take responsibility, learn from the experience and change your process to prevent that situation from happening again. A lot of the time, a simple tweak to your contract will help to prevent issues in the future.

One such lesson came about when I had a client who appeared to vanish off the face of the planet, only to return six months later as if no time had passed. As there was nothing in my contract that stated otherwise, I simply continued with the project; however, I immediately rectified this in my contract, adding a note that if the feedback is not received after thirty days, the project will be archived and an additional amount will be charged for unarchiving and commencing the project. Making that change keeps me in control.

I have met a few designers who don't make contracts and agree on everything on a handshake, although I don't recommend this approach. A contract outlines the expectations of both parties and ultimately protects you both should the worst happen.

A few years back, I worked on a naming and logo project for a business. They paid 50% upfront, were a pleasure to work with throughout the project, and the solution came together nicely. Although, when settling the final payment, my client made excuse after excuse and eventually went totally off the radar, not responding to any call, email or message for several months.

My contract states that I own the full rights to all ideas and designs presented until the final payment has been made, but they had made the mistake of formally registering the name I created. As it was a breach of contract, I was able to take the business through the UK small claims court and the final amount was settled reasonably quickly.

This is why you need a contract. So you're protected and in control when the worst happens.

INVOICES

Before starting a project, I send an invoice to the client so that they can arrange payment. I send an invoice for a 50% deposit at the start of the project, then a second invoice for the final 50% once the project is complete, which needs to be settled before I send the final files.

The invoice needs to include the following:

- A unique identification number. I organise my project folders with a simple numbering system that starts at 001, so I use the same for the invoice to help keep everything nicely organised. I'll then add an A to the first invoice and B to the second. For example, the invoice number might be 136A.

- Your name (or company name), address, email and telephone number.

- The company name and address of the customer you're invoicing.

- The date of the invoice.

- A clear description of what you're charging for.

- The amount(s) being charged.

- VAT amount, if applicable. In the UK, if you're not VAT registered, you don't need to include this.

- The total amount owed.

- I also include my bank details, as a bank transfer is my preferred payment method.

Island Health logo design by Ian Paget

At first, I designed an invoice template in InDesign, which did the job. But as I started to work on more projects, it wasn't a practical way of working. I now use dedicated accounting software, which allows me to create professional invoices quickly, while also keeping track of all my incoming and outgoing money. There are lots of options; I've listed a few at the back of this book (page 317).

SPOTTING RED FLAGS

Another benefit of talking with a business owner on the phone is that you can assess whether you'd like to work with them. How someone acts before proceeding with a project is very likely to be how they will behave throughout the project, so if there's anything that doesn't feel right, you might not want to go ahead.

Most people I've worked with have been incredible, but sadly there are unpleasant people out there who could become bad clients – the type who will be disrespectful, respond late, withhold information, seek excessive control, steal your work, or consistently delay payments. A brief phone call can help to identify early warning signs.

For example, I once had a call from someone who had a bad experience with his previous designer. I was greeted with an in-depth story about how awful things got. Yes, a designer can sometimes screw up, but that rang alarm bells for me. This guy used the designer's first name and it happened to be someone I knew. So before taking things any further, I reached out to my friend, only to find out that this particular client wanted everything at short notice. Then, when it came to paying, he'd make up excuse after excuse. I'm glad I avoided that one!

On another occasion, I had a client who asked a lot of questions on the initial call and followed up with a further list of questions before deciding to proceed. While this is understandable, after sending over a contract to start the ball rolling, he followed up with even more questions, repeating some I had already answered in detail! I sensed this would be a continuing trend throughout the project and while he might have been OK to work with, I declined the work as I didn't feel it would be worth the ongoing hassle.

Then there was the time I couldn't answer my phone because I was preparing an evening meal for my family. Rather than leave a voicemail, as an average human would, this guy rang my phone repeatedly for nearly half an hour! Imagine that person as a client!? No way.

Trust your gut. No amount of money is worth the suffering that can be endured by working for an unpleasant person, so if something doesn't feel right, run.

LEARN TO SAY NO

Not every client will be a good fit. There's a market for every buyer and that's the nature of business.

Just because someone can get a budget logo doesn't mean you need to bring your price down to match. They're not buying the same thing. If they're happy with the cheaper option, that's their choice. This is no different to getting a handbag from Primark for a few dollars and then expecting Prada to reduce their prices to match. That would be ridiculous. Yes, they're both bags, but they differ considerably in many ways. As does your logo design service! There's a market for everything. If someone can't afford you, that's fine. Wish them well and move on.

Once you've worked out your price, be confident about it. Don't reduce it because someone doesn't see the value. Others will. There will always be those who try to get a sneaky discount. It's common for service-based businesses. Some will accommodate, so knowing that wouldn't you try this too if you were a client? I don't blame them.

It's okay to say no. I'm confident in my prices. I know how I fit in the market. Clients often need us more than we need them, so if I'm asked for a discount and politely decline, they still go ahead anyway. They're just trying in the hope it might work. It's also okay to say yes, too, if you want. It's your business, your choice.

PAY YOUR TAXES

When you start making money from your skills, you need to play by a few rules. This will differ based on where you live, so I suggest doing your own research to understand the rules that will apply to you, but usually, you'll need to pay taxes on the profits that you make.

Here in the UK, you can choose to operate as a sole trader or as a limited company. To register, head to the gov.uk website or do a Google search for "set up a business."

Throughout my journey, I've operated as a sole trader, which means I'm responsible for keeping my sales and expenses records. Additionally, I'm required to complete

a self-assessment tax return annually, and pay Income Tax and National Insurance. To ensure I have the money to pay for this, I have two bank accounts – one for my business income and outgoings and a separate bank account where I transfer 30% of my monthly profits for the tax man. I suggest doing something similar, as the amount can build up once you start operating full-time, so it's helpful to have this separate from your other money so you don't get a nasty surprise each year.

I did my first self-assessment independently and found it confusing, so you might want to invest in a good accountant to help you do this properly.

Olive Global logo design by Ian Paget

PART 13

PLANNING YOUR TIME

ONCE YOU'VE SOLD A LOGO PROJECT, YOUR NEW CLIENT WILL WANT AN INDICATION OF HOW LONG EVERYTHING WILL TAKE AND WHEN THEY CAN EXPECT TO HEAR FROM YOU. SO YOU'LL NEED TO BE ABLE TO FIGURE THIS OUT.

IN THIS SECTION, I'LL SHARE THE TECHNIQUES & TOOLS I USE TO PLAN MY TIME & STAY ORGANISED.

If you're starting your journey as I did, doing everything on the side of a full-time job won't be easy. After all, there are only so many hours in the day, so it's essential to plan your time well.

My official working hours at my day job were from 9:00am to 5:30pm; however, due to the demands of my position, I frequently worked overtime. Additionally, I had a one-hour commute each way due to rush hour traffic. This meant I had to wake up at 7:00am to be ready and out the door by 8:00am. In the evenings, I would typically arrive home by 7:00pm, have dinner, and wouldn't have any free time until after 8:00pm. Therefore, the only available time I had to work on projects was from 8:00pm onwards on weekdays or during weekends.

It's easy to fill every minute of that time with work, so don't forget there are other commitments in life, such as friends and family… and for your own mental and physical health, you also need to rest. That's important.

To make it manageable, I booked only one project at a time. Keeping it simple enabled me to give myself and my clients a realistic two to three weeks time frame.

I would work between 16 to 24 hours on a logo project, so giving myself a decent timescale meant I didn't need to panic. I would do an hour or so every other evening and if needed, I could block out time during the weekends too. This enabled me to work steadily, fit everything else in and not burn myself out.

Aside from working on projects, I found pockets of time in the day for all the small tasks, such as social posting. I made it a routine to post on social media every morning to build an audience. I didn't want to miss a day.

I'll admit there were days when I didn't feel like it, but I did it anyway. It became a habit and part of my morning ritual, along with brushing my teeth, eating breakfast and putting on clothes, just one of those things I did without too much thought.

It's worth mentioning that you can schedule social posts to make the most of your available time, so I used Buffer for a period of time, which is an app designed for managing your social posts. There's plenty of other options out there, with a few listed at the back of this book (page 312).

I then started to seek out opportunities to maximise my time. One approach was to take the train to work instead of driving. Not because it was faster, but because on the train, I could post on social media and read and respond to emails. It was a much more effective use of my time compared to driving.

Everything was manageable at the beginning. A project would come in, I'd get it done, and I'd move on with my life. As things started to grow, things started to change.

I didn't factor in the time needed to respond to the new leads, phone calls, and messages that came as a result of ongoing growth. If I were to respond to each call and message, I would never have a moment to myself. This situation became increasingly stressful and overwhelming. This is why I eventually took the leap to full-time. Not so much out of choice, but because it felt inevitable. I discuss that transition later in the book (page 262).

THE TOOLS I USE TO PLAN MY TIME

Once I worked for myself full-time, I was able to manage my time more effectively. However, time will fly by without careful planning, so to help with this, I use a combination of three tools: Google Calendar, Trello, and a notebook.

GOOGLE CALENDAR

I use Google Calendar to plan time for projects from a high-level perspective. Having high-level visibility of what I have on the go means I can give clients an accurate estimate of when I will have an initial presentation ready to send.

I keep this relatively simple. For example, I'll block out Monday and Tuesday for one project, then Thursday and Friday for another. I like to leave Wednesdays free in case I need extra time on a project or if I want to work on something to help grow my business, such as writing a blog post or recording/editing a podcast. I won't schedule anything else on those days unless it's a relatively quick win, such as a client call.

I've been booked up as much as three months ahead and stay on schedule using this approach, although it's worth noting that I never cram my diary full. Unexpected things will always take up time, so I like to leave a week empty each month, intended as a "buffer."

This free time in my diary allows me to move projects around, so if I need time to put together a proposal or need more time to focus on a project, I can. Most importantly, I can easily make time for those exciting projects that might come up without causing significant delays to the projects I've already committed to.

TRELLO

As I work on multiple projects simultaneously, it's important that I know what stage I'm at with each. To have visibility of this, I use a project management application called Trello. There are many ways to use Trello, but my approach has been to create a column for each project stage. I then add a project as a Card and drag and drop it to the appropriate column as the project progresses.

The columns I use are:

- Goals to Write

- Design Phase

- Presentation Sent

- Updates to Make

- Create Files

- Awaiting Payment

Once the final payment has been made and the files sent, I will archive the card.

Passcomm

...making the connection

Passcomm logo design by Ian Paget

If you work on other types of projects, you can add separate boards to keep track of the appropriate steps. For example, I use another for podcasting. It's super simple and works well.

There's an abundance of alternate project management applications available, depending on your preference, including Monday, Wrike and Asana to name a few.

A NOTEBOOK

Lastly, I use a physical notebook to list all the individual tasks. There's a long list of digital tools that perform the same thing, but I like the speed and practicality of keeping a handwritten list. Plus, I like the sheer satisfaction of crossing things off my list. It's a nice way to see that I'm making progress daily.

I'm well aware though that a long list can become overwhelming. When working in an agency as Design Director, I quickly became inundated with tasks. Some tasks were requested via an internal management system, and I had several verbal requests from managers too. To help keep track, I started to keep a written to-do list so I wouldn't miss anything. Although, there were days when I'd have so many tasks that my to-do list would stretch across three or four pages of A4 paper, making me feel incredibly stressed.

I realised, however, that not all tasks have the same level of priority. Most tasks could wait a few days and some were long-term ideas. To help the list feel more manageable, I would grab a highlighter pen and pick out the most urgent tasks that needed to be done that day.

Usually, this would narrow a list of fifty items to just a few, making it comfortably manageable.

Once the most urgent tasks on my list were complete, I'd either finish for the day or start working on the task of my choice, this could be the next project on my list, or something business-related such as writing a case study.

Occasionally, there were days when I highlighted more tasks than I could physically do in the time I had. In those cases, I would number them in priority order. Those at the top of the list were the tasks for the most important clients or those of the highest value. Those lower down the list would need to wait, so if I knew it was very unlikely that I would complete a task that day, I could at least set expectations as early as possible with the necessary people.

I still use this approach daily, and it allows me to keep track of every little task to ensure it's completed.

This straightforward approach has worked well for me. However, there's a wide variety of digital tools and applications out there to assist with project management depending on your personal preference. Explore the options available, and use those that work best for you and your needs.

PART 14

GOING FULL-TIME

ONCE YOU'VE MASTERED THE ART OF LOGO DESIGN, ATTRACTED CLIENTS & ESTABLISHED A REPUTATION, YOU'RE READY TO WORK FOR YOURSELF FULL-TIME.

IN THIS SECTION, I'LL SHARE THE JOURNEY THAT I TOOK TO GO FROM BEING A HOBBYIST DESIGNER TO BECOMING A FULL-TIME PROFESSIONAL LOGO DESIGNER.

Throughout this book, I have shared my design process and details of how I attract clients, sell my services and continue to build my reputation. So as a summary, I shall end the book with an overview of my journey from hobbyist to full-time professional logo designer.

I hope that sharing this will help cement some of the ideas discussed throughout this book to help you with your journey to make a living designing logos.

STARTING MY DESIGN BUSINESS

By the time I made the decision to launch my own business, I'd already gained professional experience by working on logo design projects in my full-time position. However, due to contractual obligations, I was unable to use any of that work to attract clients. Unless the contract says otherwise, when designing something for an agency, it's the intellectual property of that company. This meant that creating examples in my own time was essential to attract potential clients for my business.

The first logos I designed were for friends and family. Most of these I did free of charge to practice while building up my portfolio. There's a lot of negative press about working for free, which is understandable if you're being taken advantage of, although, when you're new to design, those portfolio pieces and positive testimonials are of great value to you, so it's a mutually beneficial trade.

I built a simple website to display my work. Once I had decided on a name, I registered the domain and had a site live and ready to share within a couple of days.

Sharing the website on my social profiles attracted projects from old school friends and work colleagues who became my first paying clients. I charged very little, but since I had a full-time job, I was excited about the extra disposable income. This sparked excitement as I realised I could attract more paying clients if I worked for it.

BUILDING A REPUTATION

To promote my newfound hobby, I created a Facebook business page to share my work and the valuable logo design resources I discovered. This didn't perform as I had expected. Instead, I attracted a small following of other designers. But I enjoyed finding and sharing design resources. As I treated my business as a hobby, I continued regardless, as it was a practical way to keep track of the resources I discovered and the lessons I learned.

In my full-time position, we hired someone to manage the company's social media. This is where I picked up a few tips for building a following on Twitter. After this, I took the content I was already sharing on Facebook and shared it on Twitter too. I worked on this every day and gradually built a following.

I continued to add more work examples to my website. I wrote about the lessons I learned and continued sharing resources on social media daily. This allowed me to be seen by outsiders as an expert.

I started to be invited to juries for awards and asked to contribute to design blogs, which helped to build my reputation as a logo designer. Each opportunity provided a high-quality link to my website, helping to improve my visibility on Google.

Through this ongoing effort, I started to attract enquiries from people outside of my network. At first, those enquiries were few and far between, however, I continued to work on my website for several years. I slowly improved my site during evenings, weekends and holidays, adding more content, case studies and blog posts.

Whenever I had time to relax and unwind, I enjoyed working on my website. It was a hobby, and I never intended for the business to become more than just a fun side project. My ultimate career goal was to move up the ladder at design companies, and I liked to continually advance my skills, so I would work on fun and exciting side projects as a way to test and learn and develop. This was meant to be just another one of those projects.

Logo Geek blossomed into much more than a hobby. It dramatically changed my life and career more than I ever imagined.

DECIDING MY FUTURE

What began as the occasional enquiry turned into several leads a week… then several a day. I would have been swamped if I had converted all the leads that came my way, however, with a full-time job keeping me occupied, I didn't have time to respond to every enquiry, let alone do the work too.

It became overwhelming. I felt like I had created a monster that would continue to grow and consume every aspect of my life unless I pulled the plug. So I needed to make a decision. Do I keep my job and continue to work up the corporate ladder as I had always imagined? Or do I leap into uncertainty and work for myself?

I've always enjoyed operating within a team. I like sharing and discussing ideas, collaborating with others and focusing on the tasks allocated to me. I also liked the guaranteed income of a full-time job and the ability to be "free" in the evenings and weekends. In comparison, the thought of working for myself was terrifying. I'd need to do everything from sales, accounts, design and presentations to marketing and processes… it's a lot of pressure.

The comfortable decision was to continue to work for a design agency and pull the plug on what I had started. Although, I had worked so hard on building Logo Geek, and had seen so much success, I did not want to pull the plug. It was like killing my baby.

Rocks & Roads logo design by Ian Paget

However, that didn't solve the issue. If I carried on as I was, I would be forever stressed, juggling too many balls simultaneously. I was stuck in a rut.

I continued working in my day job and kept Logo Geek going in my free time, even though I felt burnt out. This was hurting other areas of my life too, as it affected not only me but those around me.

There were other things on my mind as well. My mum had been diagnosed with vascular dementia, and each time I went to visit, she was fading away. After several small strokes, she had lost the ability to walk and eventually the ability to swallow...

Days later, she passed away.

My mum was cared for in a specialist dementia home, so I met many other people who were shadows of who they once were. This was the end of their story.

I thought to myself that I would never want to get to that point in my life having regrets. It pushed me to reflect on my life and I knew I was letting my fears prevent me from progressing and living my life fully. Logo Geek was one of those things. What if I did pull the plug and never got to see where I could take it? I know I would regret it forever.

From that day on, I did things differently. I started to do the things that scared me because I knew deep down that I could make them work. Where I once said no, I now say yes. I had to, or I'd regret it.

A PART-TIME STEP

I decided to give my notice and focus on Logo Geek full-time. This was daunting, but I had the enquiries coming in, and I knew I could make it work. I also knew that if I screwed up, I could search for a new job. To satisfy my contract, I needed to give two months' notice. This would give me time to start booking in projects, so I'd have plenty on the go once I had left. So I wrote a resignation letter and met with my boss the following day.

To my surprise, they were very supportive of my ambitions. As I had been at the company for several years and had become an integral part of the business, they asked if I would consider working part-time. This was ideal. It gave me the time I needed to work on my own projects while providing the security of a guaranteed monthly income.

I agreed to cut back to three days a week, giving me the rest of the week to work on my business. This allowed me to go from taking on the occasional project to working on three or four logo design projects per month. I also had time to work on other business areas that would help further establish my reputation as a logo designer, such as a podcast and building a community.

Going part-time worked out for the best. I think I would have failed if I hadn't transitioned slowly. I needed time to find my bearings as a business owner. At first, I didn't enjoy it as much as I had hoped. This was primarily because I had to spend most of my time focusing on the areas of my business that made money, not on the things I was excited about and wanted to work on.

I know that sounds obvious, but I imagined that I would suddenly have more time to work on the aspects of the business that excited me, such as revamping my website, adding more case studies and writing more consistently. However, none of this makes money directly, so it's never an immediate priority.

I was also less motivated than I thought and a little lazy. For the previous fifteen years, working for others, I had been an early riser and worked hard every hour of every day. I pictured that I would continue to wake up at 6:30am, head to the gym, and then crank out work from 9:00am until 6:00pm with a midday lunch break. That sadly didn't happen.

I no longer had a boss and was finally free! So when that alarm went off, I could hit that snooze button and sleep a little longer, even though I knew I shouldn't… it was just nice to have that choice. Although, that meant I started late.

I was also easily distracted by things like social media. It was tempting because I had the freedom to check it whenever I wanted, which was something I couldn't do when working for someone else. However, this resulted in wasted time.

I also had difficulty in maintaining a clear boundary between work and personal life. Household tasks that I might have left until the evening became distractions. I told myself that I would have to do them eventually anyway, so why not now? As a result, my focus suffered.

I also found it rather lonely working for myself, as there was no one to brainstorm ideas with, seek advice from, or share moments of success with.

I wasn't sure if I was up to the task.

Blue Inspirations logo design by Ian Paget

MAKING IT WORK

Despite the initial rocky start, I persevered and worked out practical ways to solve my problems.

I hired a desk at a nearby co-working space, where I set up my computer and everything else I needed to get the job done. Although this had a monthly cost, it helped me to feel more serious about the business. It also gave me a routine similar to the one I was used to. I'd get up on time, get dressed and take a short walk before starting my day. It also allowed me to meet other people rather than being alone at home.

As the weeks passed, I noticed I didn't need to be so hard on myself. I realised that I didn't need to work as hard or as long as I had been used to while working for an agency. I no longer needed to juggle multiple projects and tasks, as I had become used to. I could instead focus on just one task, do it very well, and still get paid well.

I also had the flexibility to work when I wanted. For instance, I could work from 7:00am to 12:00pm, take a break, and then resume at 7:00pm later in the day – it was entirely my decision. As long as I accomplished the tasks, the specific time I worked didn't matter. If I felt the need for more rest in the morning, I allowed it. Likewise, if I wanted to work late, I had the freedom to do so. If I ever wanted to stop early, and my schedule allowed for it, I could wrap things up for the day.

I started to feel in control. I was calmer and happier. Yes, it took time, but I eventually got used to the new lifestyle I had created. I made it work.

THE BIGGER PICTURE

Now that I felt more settled, I began looking at the bigger picture. I realised that if I could reduce my living costs, I would have higher profits.

At that point, I was renting a lovely city centre flat with an easy commute to London, which came at a premium. Buying a property in that area was an impossible task. But in the North of the country, property prices were significantly lower.

The company where I worked part-time had a small Northern office, so I asked if I could work from that office instead. They agreed. That meant I could move. Plus, because property prices were low in that area, I could get a mortgage on a nice three-bedroom house with a large back garden and a private driveway. The overall monthly cost was almost half what I had been paying for rent, so not only did I get on the property ladder and have more space, I also gave myself a monthly pay raise.

I turned the biggest bedroom into a dedicated office, where I could close the door, and the rest of the house was for living. Although this meant I needed to give up the office space, by that point, I was starting to get used to working for myself and was comfortable working from home. I just needed time to adjust.

I became much more relaxed and set realistic goals, making the experience more enjoyable.

TAKING THE LEAP

Three years had passed before I considered seriously leaping to full-time. The thought of doing so actually terrified me.

Then my daughter was born.

Whenever I was away from home, I would be sent photos of her and I felt I was missing out. I wanted to be there. I wanted to watch my little one grow up and be an active part of her life.

I also noticed that I was never entirely 100% committed to either my part-time role or my logo design business. Although I had a guaranteed income, my part-time position had no room for growth. I was in the highest role possible and any further development required full-time commitment. And in my own business, knowing I had a financial safety net, I never worked as hard as I could have.

I was comfortable, but not making progress.

A change was needed.

That was when I started to work out how much I would need to earn in my own business to match my part-time salary. I'd never considered working out how much I earned daily before then. I only looked at my annual salary and thought I was well paid. But to my surprise, it was much less than I had thought.

I only needed to book two or three extra projects per month to replace that income. Not only did that sound comfortably doable, it also left me regretting that I hadn't worked this out sooner.

What provided me with more comfort was the fact that I had almost four months' worth of salary saved in my bank account. In the worst-case scenario, I could cover my living expenses for several months. If I realised it wasn't working out, I would have the time to search for a new job. I felt secure. So I made the decision. I was going to fully commit. The time had come! I gave two months' notice and immediately focused on the transition.

I worked harder than ever before, working every waking hour. I booked in as many projects as I could. I redesigned my website. I did everything possible to ensure my new full-time venture would thrive. And it did.

After two months of being my own boss, I received a call from the University of Cambridge to work on a logo project. To get a call from such a reputable organisation blew my mind. I never expected it to happen, however, somehow I managed to secure the job, and I've been fortunate enough to work with them other logo projects.

If I hadn't made the leap to full-time when I did, I'm confident this would have never happened. The updates I made to my website played a significant role, although most importantly, I now had time to take calls, prepare proposals, respond quickly and be reactive about deliverable times. I could finally be the professional I wanted to be.

I've continued working with great clients and love what I do. What started as a hobby became a passion, which developed into a business... and that enabled me to make a living doing what I love most – designing logos.

And that's not even the most significant benefit of this journey... One of the greatest joys of building Logo Geek is that I can work from home and witness my daughter growing up. It's priceless to have the opportunity to create precious memories with her, which would have been impossible if I did not build my own business.

This journey is unique to me and is far from its end, but I hope the experiences and lessons shared throughout this book have provided the inspiration and motivation you need to start your journey as a logo designer.

We're near the end of the book, however, I don't want things to end here. I hope it's clear that everyone works differently and has their own story to tell, which is why I will continue to interview successful logo designers, entrepreneurs and business owners through *The Logo Geek Podcast* so we can collectively learn from as many people as possible. I hope you'll listen along and find the conversations valuable and inspiring.

There's no single way to make a living as a logo designer, so learn from as many people as possible to discover what works for you. I wish you all the best with your new adventure and look forward to hearing your success story when you're ready.

Synergy logo design by Ian Paget

PART 15

FURTHER LEARNING & SUPPORT

This book has been written to be a starting point for you to learn logo design and make a living from your newfound skills. To help you continue learning, in this section, I've listed several incredible books, resources and tools that have been useful throughout my journey.

I have included a link with each resource to help you quickly find it. In some cases, these are affiliate links, meaning if you visit the link and make a purchase, I will receive a commission at no extra cost.

These recommendations are based on my experience, and I share them only because I believe they will be genuinely useful, not because of a small commission I may receive. Please only spend money on something if it will help you achieve your goals.

I keep this list updated digitally with the latest and greatest tools. To view this, head to:

LOGOGEEK.UK/RESOURCES

LOGO GEEK PODCAST

To supplement this book, I host *The Logo Geek Podcast*. Each episode features an interview with a guest and covers a wide range of topics, including logo design (obviously), brand strategy, client relationships, marketing and more.

At the time of releasing this book, there are 150 episodes to dive into, featuring prominent industry names, including Sagi Haviv, Emily Oberman, Marty Neumeier, Aaron Draplin and many other inspiring individuals.

To listen to the podcast, head to **logogeek.uk/podcast**, or search on your preferred podcasting platform.

Here are a few of my favourite episodes to get started:

- *Saying No to Clients with Sagi Haviv.* Listen @ **logogeek.uk/22**

- *Designing Identities for TV & Film, an Interview with Emily Oberman.* Listen @ **logogeek.uk/98**

- *How To Get Logo Design Clients with Tom Ross & Michael Janda.* Listen @ **logogeek.uk/90**

- *A Life of Food & Restaurant Branding with Louise Fili.* Listen @ **logogeek.uk/30**

- *A Masterclass in Logo Design Theory with Michael Shumate.* Listen @ **logogeek.uk/84**

LOGO TALK ZINE

While many people may not have the luxury of dedicating time to listen to podcasts, I'm determined to ensure that the valuable insights from the guests of *The Logo Geek Podcast* reach as many people as possible.

To accomplish this goal, I have created the *Logo Talk* Zine, which showcases lightly edited transcripts of the podcast's best interviews.

Available print on demand globally through Amazon.

logogeek.uk/logotalk

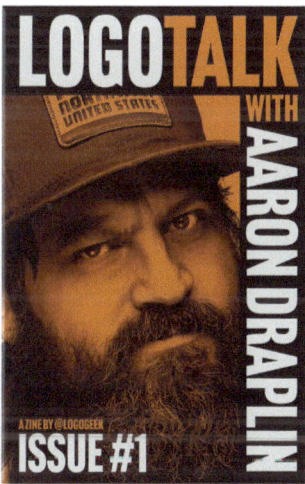

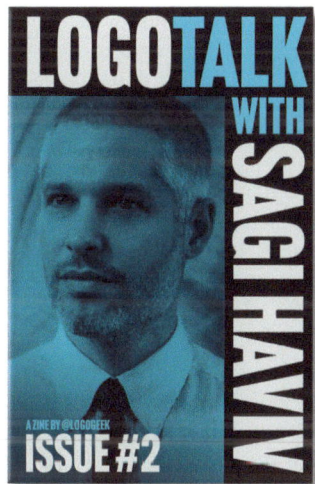

COMMUNITY

If you're a designer looking for a community of like-minded individuals, I'm on a mission to help.

First of all, I've created *The Logo Geek Community* on Facebook, which is free to join! With over 10,000 members from around the globe, it's a great place to ask questions, get feedback and discuss everything logo design. logogeek.uk/community

In addition to this, I have created *Logo Geek Logo Club*, built upon Circle, a platform made for communities. Away from the distraction and noise of Facebook, this has been created to be a fun, safe environment to support those serious about making a living from logo design. logogeek.uk/club

LIVE HANGOUTS

If you want to hang out with me and a group of like-minded designers on live video calls, I've created *Logo Geek Hangouts*, part of *Logo Geek Logo Club*, which has been designed to replicate the casual design community meetups at events in big cities.

I believe in the power of a tight-knit community where everyone knows and trusts one another; that's why the hangouts are invite-only. But don't worry, if you would like to be considered as a member, please send an introductory email to ian@logogeek.com

BOOKS

As a logo design enthusiast, I've amassed a vast collection of books on logo design, branding, graphic design, and business. If you're also looking to improve your design and business skills, I've categorised the most helpful books from my collection to aid you on your journey.

Choosing which books to buy from those listed here will likely be overwhelming, so to help you out, I've narrowed it down to my top 5 recommendations for an all-round education in logo design, branding and business. In addition to this, I've added a star next to the rest that I feel are a must read.

TOP 5 BOOKS FOR AN ALL-ROUND EDUCATION

1. LOGO MODERNISM

You'll want to include at least one gallery reference book for inspiration in your collection.

There are plenty out there, but "*Logo Modernism*" by Jens Müller and R. Roger Remington is the one that rules them all. It's a HUGE book packed with so much logo inspiration that you'll never need to buy another.

To buy, head to: logogeek.uk/books1

2. LOGO CREED

I recommend having at least one book about the logo design process. Among the various options available (including the one you're reading now), "*Logo Creed*" by Bill Gardner is a great choice.

Its research section is particularly useful, and it offers in-depth case studies from some of the world's best logo designers.

To buy, head to: logogeek.uk/books2

3. TYPE MATTERS

Typography is a fundamental element of logo design. However, if you start editing or creating your own letterforms without an understanding of type design, your work will inevitably appear amateurish. Therefore, gaining an understanding of the intricacies of type design is essential for learning logo design.

This topic is a rabbit hole, so as a primer, I highly recommend "*Type Matters*" by Jim Williams. It's a beautifully designed book that will give you a solid foundation to typography design.

To buy, head to: logogeek.uk/books3

4. DESIGNING BRAND IDENTITY

In isolation, designing a logo might sound simple, but to excel at the job, you must grasp the essence of the brand it represents. Therefore, it's crucial to have at least one book on branding.

There are numerous excellent books available on branding and brand strategy, but if you're starting with just one, I recommend "*Designing Brand Identity*" by Alina Wheeler. This was one of the first design books I purchased and remains a favourite that I frequently reference. It will provide you with a comprehensive understanding of every aspect of the branding process, complete with helpful diagrams throughout.

To buy, head to: logogeek.uk/books4

5. BURN YOUR PORTFOLIO

To become a successful designer, you'll need to cultivate various interpersonal and business skills alongside your design acumen. Therefore, I recommend having at least one business book in your collection.

A great starting point is "*Burn Your Portfolio*" by Michael Janda. In this book, he shares real-world practices, professional do's and don'ts, and the unwritten rules of business that most designers only learn after years of experience.

To buy, head to: logogeek.uk/books5

LOGO GALLERY BOOKS

- *Logo Modernism* by Jens Müller and R. Roger Remington ⭐
  logogeek.uk/books1

- *Identity: Chermayeff & Geismar & Haviv* ⭐
  logogeek.uk/books6

- *Logo: The Reference Guide to Symbols and Logotypes* by Michael Evamy
  logogeek.uk/books7

- *Pentagram: Marks*
  logogeek.uk/books8

- *Trade Marks & Symbols* by Yasaburo Kuwayama
  logogeek.uk/books9

- *Logo-A-GoGo: Branding Pop Culture* by Rian Hughes
  logogeek.uk/books10

- *Brand by Hand: Blisters, Calluses, and Clients: A Life in Design* by Jon Contino
  logogeek.uk/books11

- *Draplin Design Co.: Pretty Much Everything* by Aaron James Draplin ⭐
  logogeek.uk/books12

LOGO PROCESS BOOKS

- *Logo Creed: The Mystery, Magic, and Method Behind Designing Great Logos* by Bill Gardner ★
  logogeek.uk/books2

- *Logo Design Love: A Guide to Creating Iconic Brand Identities* by David Airey ★
  logogeek.uk/books13

- *Smashing Logo Design: The Art of Creating Visual Identities* by Gareth Hardy
  logogeek.uk/books14

LOGO INFORMATION BOOKS

- *TM: The Untold Stories Behind 29 Classic Logos* by Mark Sinclair
  logogeek.uk/books15

- *Logo Life: Life Histories of 100 Famous Logos* by Ron van der Vlugt
  logogeek.uk/books16

- *The Logo Design Idea Book* by Gail Anderson and Steven Heller
  logogeek.uk/books17

- *Marks of Excellence: The History and Taxonomy of Trademarks* by Per Mollerup
  logogeek.uk/books18

- *Design, Form and Chaos* by Paul Rand ★
  logogeek.uk/books19

BRAND & STRATEGY BOOKS

- *Designing Brand Identity: An Essential Guide for the Whole Branding Team* by Alina Wheeler ★
  logogeek.uk/books4

- *The Brand Gap: How to Bridge the Distance Between Business Strategy and Design* by Marty Neumeier
  logogeek.uk/books20

- *ZAG: The Number One Strategy of High-Performance Brands* by Marty Neumeier ★
  logogeek.uk/books21

- *The Brand Flip: Why Customers Now Run Companies and How to Profit from it* by Marty Neumeier
  logogeek.uk/books22

- *Branding: In Five and a Half Steps* by Michael Johnson
  logogeek.uk/books23

- *Brand New Name: A Proven, Step-by-Step Process to Create an Unforgettable Brand Name* by Jeremy Miller
  logogeek.uk/books24

TYPOGRAPHY BOOKS

- *Type Matters!* by Jim Williams ★
  logogeek.uk/books3

- *How to Create Typefaces: From Sketch to Screen* by Cristóbal Henestrosa, José Scaglione, and Laura Meseguer
  logogeek.uk/books25

- *Fonts & Logos* by Doyald Young
  logogeek.uk/books26

- *Why Fonts Matter* by Sarah Hyndman ★
  logogeek.uk/books27

COLOUR THEORY BOOKS

- *Color Works: Best Practices for Graphic Designers* by
  Eddie Opara and John Cantwell ★
  logogeek.uk/books28

- *The Designer's Dictionary of Colour* by Sean Adams
  logogeek.uk/books29

- *The Secret Lives of Colour* by Kassia St. Clair
  logogeek.uk/books30

BUSINESS BOOKS

- *Burn Your Portfolio* by Michael Janda ★
  logogeek.uk/books5

- *Pricing Creativity* by Blair Enns ★
  logogeek.uk/books31

- *Work for Money, Design for Love* by David Airey ★
  logogeek.uk/books32

- *The One Thing* by Gary Keller and Jay Papasan
  logogeek.uk/books33

- *The E-Myth Revisited* by Michael E. Gerber ★
  logogeek.uk/books34

TRAINING COURSES

In today's world of endless digital possibilities, learning something new has become easier than ever before. From YouTube to podcasts, there's a vast supply of free resources available for anyone looking to gain knowledge.

That being said, sometimes it can be exhausting to sift through all the information out there and knowing what's reliable. This is where courses come in handy! They can save you time by bringing together all the essential information in one convenient location.

LOGO COURSES

- **Logo Design: From Concept to Presentation** by Sagi Haviv. This is published through Domestika, and at the time of releasing this book, it's a bargain at under $20.
  logogeek.uk/course1

- **Design a Logo in Modern Style** by George Bokhua (Published through SkillShare)
  logogeek.uk/course2

- **Logo Design with Grids: Timeless Style from Simple Shapes** by George Bokhua (Published through SkillShare)
  logogeek.uk/course3

- **Logo Design with Draplin:** Secrets of Shape, Type and Color by Aaron Draplin (Published through SkillShare)
  logogeek.uk/course4

- **Adobe Illustrator CC: Advanced Training.** Although this isn't strictly logo design, if you're purely looking for a course to help master the tools, I highly recommend training by Daniel Scott, and for just $12 per month, you'll gain access to his entire library of courses.
logogeek.uk/course5

- **Logo Core Masterclass.** This isn't one I've personally taken, yet I feel it is worth mentioning here since it's the most comprehensive logo design course that I've come across. Prices start from $100.
logogeek.uk/course6

- **Logo Design 01** by the Futur. The most expensive option on this list at $149; however, Chris Do is a superb educator who explains the process well.
logogeek.uk/course7

BRAND STRATEGY COURSES

- **Logo & Brand Design Process: Behind The Scenes** by Jacob Cass. This course is ideal if you want to provide a more valuable service, designing identities based on brand strategy. At the time of releasing this book, it's only $29, too, so a real bargain.
logogeek.uk/course8

- **Brand Master Secrets** by Stephen Houraghan. This is the most comprehensive Brand Strategy Course out there, so if you're considering going deeper on the topic, this is worth a look. It's priced at $897, but you'll be working through the content for some time.
logogeek.uk/course9

- **Level C.** If you're eager to delve deeper into brand strategy, I highly recommend Level C, which proudly describes itself as the world's most visionary brand education program.

  It's founded by (and also partly taught by) the legendary Marty Neumeier and is broken down into numerous levels, eventually qualifying you to become a Chief Branding Officer, which in some companies is a job that pays 7 figures.

  Unlike the other courses listed here, this isn't simply a set of pre-recorded videos. It's a live and interactive workshop, so not only are you taught by pros, but you'll also get to collaborate on projects with some brilliant people.

  This is as intense as it gets with the courses listed here and it comes with a high price tag, however, if you want to learn from the best in the business in a live environment and become a Certified Brand Strategist in the process, then this is the course to take.

  logogeek.uk/course10

FREELANCE COURSES

There's only one freelancing course I'd like to recommend in this book: "**The Ultimate Freelance Course**" by Michael Janda. I can't stress enough how remarkable this course is. I would go so far as to say that I consider it an essential course to take if you're truly committed to making a living as a designer.

There are many courses on topics that this course covers, but what makes this special is Michael. He's been there, done it, and made a lot of money doing it, too. He's more interested in providing value and helping people than making money.

His advice is real… it's practical… it's priceless.

The course includes 40+ hours of video lessons and comes with proposal templates, contracts, pricing systems, project management templates, and more.

It's not cheap, selling at $399+, although it's incredibly comprehensive, full of real-world, practical advice, and well-presented. It's worth… every… penny.

logogeek.uk/course11

OTHER COURSES

When you work for yourself, there's loads of stuff you can learn to grow as an individual. To help with that, here are a few excellent low-cost educational platforms I've used for work and play:

- **Domestika**   logogeek.uk/domestika

- **SkillShare**   logogeek.uk/skillshare

- **LinkedIn Learning** logogeek.uk/linkedin-learning

- **Creative Live**   logogeek.uk/creative-live

DESIGN STUFF

DESIGN SOFTWARE & EXTENSIONS

- **Adobe Illustrator.** The industry standard tool for creating vector graphics, and the software I use for logo design.
  logogeek.uk/software1

- **Astute Graphics.** A collection of plugins for Adobe Illustrator that extend the software's features to streamline and improve the workflow. I use the Smart Remove Brush Tool, part of the VectorScribe plugin, on every project to refine and perfect my logo artwork for a professional finish.
  logogeek.uk/software2

- **Logo Package Express.** An extension for Adobe Illustrator that allows you to easily create a comprehensive package of logo files. I use this on every logo project as it saves hours compared to doing it manually. It's a must-have tool for a professional logo designer.
  logogeek.uk/software3

- **Logo Package Portal.** A really nice platform from the creators of Logo Package Express that allows your clients to quickly find the correct logo file for their project. It's not something I personally use, but it deserves a mention here.
  logogeek.uk/software4

- **Affinity Designer.** An excellent alternative to Adobe Illustrator that's becoming more popular with designers due to its one-off fee.
  logogeek.uk/software5

- **Inkscape.** A free and open-source vector graphics editor.
  logogeek.uk/software6

- **Adobe Fresco.** A painting and drawing app for touchscreen devices, including mobile and tablet. You'll need an Adobe login, but the basic features are free and ideal for sketching ideas on the go.
  logogeek.uk/software7

- **Procreate.** This is the most powerful digital illustration app out there, designed for iPad and iPhone. So if you want to do more than sketch, and want a depth of features for digital painting, it's worth the one-off fee.
  logogeek.uk/software8

- **AstroPad.** This allows you to turn your iPad into a professional drawing tablet.
  logogeek.uk/software9

LOGO/DESIGN & BRANDING NEWS BLOGS

When designing logos for a living, you'll want to keep up with the latest logo design and branding news. Here's a list of websites that I personally keep an eye on:

- **logodesignlove.com**

- **logo-designer.co**

- **identitydesigned.com**

- **bpando.org**

- **underconsideration.com/brandnew**
  (it's worth the subscription)

- **creativebloq.com**

- **designweek.co.uk**

- **designtaxi.com**

- **justcreative.com/blog**

- **imjustcreative.com/blog**

- **logolounge.com/trend-reports**

- **worldbranddesign.com**

LOGO DESIGN GALLERIES

Logo design galleries offer inspiration, but you can contribute your work in many cases too. Here are some I've used:

- **logolounge.com**
  A vast collection of logos submitted by designers worldwide, serving as an inspiration and reference hub. It costs $100 a year, however, any logo you add gets considered for inclusion in their books.

- **logo-archive.org**
  A growing archive of modernist logos categorised and tagged to inspire, educate and encourage best practices in logo design.

- **logopond.com**

- **logomoose.com**

- **behance.net**
  Although not a gallery, Behance is one of the best places to look if you're seeking design inspiration.

- **dribbble.com**
  Again, not a gallery but full of inspiring design work.

COLOUR RESOURCES

- **Coolors.** If you're looking for colour palette inspiration, this website generates a palette in seconds! And if the first option doesn't quite suit your fancy, simply hit the space bar for a new one. You can also browse a list of trending colour palettes.
  coolors.co

- **Adobe Color.** A free tool that helps you to create custom colour palettes. It offers several options, including using a colour wheel with harmony rules and extracting colours from images. It's also integrated with Adobe Creative Cloud, so you can easily access your colour themes in Adobe Illustrator and more.
  color.adobe.com

- **Swatchos.** If you want to design colour palettes away from the computer, you'll enjoy using Swatchos, a deck of 129 cards created to help you choose colour schemes. The creator, Andy Brown, was a guest on the Logo Geek Podcast to discuss his creation! (Listen @ logogeek.uk/102)
  logogeek.uk/swatchos

- **Pantone Swatch books.** An essential tool for designers who work with colour. The books contain a collection of colour samples, each with a unique identification number, making it easy to communicate and reproduce colours accurately across all mediums. You'll want a Pantone Solid Coated and Uncoated book, and I recommend getting the Colour Bridge type, which includes a CMYK swatch alongside the Pantone. logogeek.uk/pantone

- **Color for Creatives.** If you're looking for a training course, Greg Gunn and the team at The Futur have created a superb course that teaches you to understand and use colour effectively. logogeek.uk/color-for-creatives

BRANDING MOCKUPS

Branding mockups are a key part of presenting logos to clients, so you'll always be on the lookout for top-quality resources. Here are a few websites that I've used:

- **Live Surface.** An incredible illustrator plugin that allows you to create realistic mockups of your designs on various elements, including billboards, clothing, and stationery, with ease and speed. logogeek.uk/mockup1

- **Place It.** A website from Envato that allows you to drop your designs onto thousands of high-quality mockup images. They have videos too, which can really bring your work to life. logogeek.uk/mockup2

- **Yellow Images.** Superb quality, high-resolution Photoshop branding mockups. You can buy just the images you need, which is what I tend to do, or if you're a heavy user, they have a subscription model which gives significant discounts.
  logogeek.uk/mockup3

- **Pixeden.** More great quality PSD branding mockups, and for only $6 a month (when paying yearly), you can download anything from their library.
  logogeek.uk/mockup4

- **Graphic Burger.** Loads of PSD mockups and design resources, but this time, they're free for both personal and commercial use.
  logogeek.uk/mockup5

- **Freebiesbug.** A collection of free design resources, including branding mockups.
  logogeek.uk/mockup6

- **Pixel Buddha.** A collection of free and premium design resources, including branding mockups.
  logogeek.uk/mockup7

- **Freepik.** Mockups and assets, free and premium.
  logogeek.uk/mockup8

- **MockupFree**. Unlimited free mockups for both personal and commercial use.
  logogeek.uk/mockup9

- **Creative Market.** Thousands of high-quality design mockups and design resources which are often sold in bundles.
  logogeek.uk/mockup10

- **Design Cuts.** Thousands of quality design assets, including branding mockups. From time to time, they offer large bundles at hugely discounted prices, with an extended commercial licence included.
logogeek.uk/mockup11

FONTS

While a quick Google search will help you find a list of font foundries and designers, I prefer to rely on a select few websites. This includes the following:

- **Adobe Fonts.** If you have an Adobe Creative Cloud subscription, this comes included.
logogeek.uk/font1

- **Google Fonts.** Over 1500 font families, freely available for commercial use.
logogeek.uk/font2

- **My Fonts.** A digital fonts distributor with the largest selection of professional fonts.
logogeek.uk/font3

- **Font Squirrel.** A curated collection of free fonts for commercial use.
logogeek.uk/font4

- **Design Cuts.** Among the treasures on this website are premium fonts, often bundled together at unbeatable prices.
logogeek.uk/font5

- **WhatTheFont.** A valuable tool for font identification.
  logogeek.uk/font6

- **Fontspring Matcherator.** Another useful font tool for identifying fonts.
  logogeek.uk/font7

- **FontBase.** An excellent free font management tool.
  logogeek.uk/font8

FICTIONAL DESIGN BRIEFS

If you're new to designing logos, you may be searching for a design brief to guide your work.

While I recommend contacting local businesses or charities and offering your services in exchange for a testimonial, you can also practice your skills with fictional logo design briefs.

Here are a few websites that offer excellent resources for this purpose:

- **Daily Logo Challenge.**
  logogeek.uk/brief1

- **Logo Core Logo Challenge.**
  logogeek.uk/brief2

- **Briefbox.**
  logogeek.uk/brief3

DESIGN AWARDS

As designers we often strive for recognition, making design awards an attractive pursuit. Winning one will boost the confidence of potential clients, position you at the forefront of excellence, and open doors to new opportunities. Being a judge on these awards will also establish you as a knowledgeable expert in your field.

Here a few awards that I've been involved with over the course of my career, either as a participant or as a judge:

- **Logo Wave.** Founded by my good friend Kyle Courtright, who's worked hard to build a reputable award for logo designers, worthy of my full support! Your work will be judged by some of the biggest names in the industry, including David Airey, Alina Wheeler, Bill Gardner, and me too. logogeek.uk/awards1

- **The International Visual Identity Awards.** A competition that recognises outstanding visual identity design from around the world, with categories ranging from corporate branding to packaging design. Use promo code LOGOGEEK for 10% off. logogeek.uk/awards2

- **The Best Brand Awards.** An international competition that gives recognition to the best logo and identity design work from around the globe. logogeek.uk/awards3

- **Transform Awards.** A competition to celebrate outstanding brand work from across the globe, highlighting the most innovative, creative, and

successful branding campaigns. I've been lucky enough to be a judge for these awards, and the entries received are truly phenomenal! Winning a Transform "Butterfly" Award is no small feat, with some of the biggest design agencies entering, and a prestigious in-person event held to give out the awards too.
logogeek.uk/awards4

- **Contest Watchers.** A website dedicated to creative challenges and design competitions worldwide.
logogeek.uk/awards5

DESIGNERS & AGENCIES

If you're keen to become the best, it's always good to take inspiration from those who have already achieved greatness. That's why I'd like to share a list of designers, creatives and agencies that inspire me:

- **Chermayeff & Geismar & Haviv**
cghnyc.com

- **David Airey**
davidairey.com

- **Ben Loiz**
benloiz.com

- **George Bokhua**
instagram.com/george_bokhua

- **Aaron Draplin**
draplin.com

- **Jacob Cass**
  justcreative.com

- **Michael Beirut**
  pentagram.com/about/michael-bierut

- **Allan Peters**
  petersdesigncompany.com

- **Louise Fili**
  louisefili.com

- **Kyle Courtright**
  courtrightdesign.com

- **James Martin**
  themadebyjames.com

- **Emily Oberman**
  pentagram.com/about/emily-oberman

- **Tamari Chabukiani**
  instagram.com/tamari.chabukiani

- **Meg Lewis**
  meglewis.com

- **Ian Barnard**
  ianbarnard.co

- **Lauren Hom**
  homsweethom.com

- **Ashwin Chacko**
  whackochacko.com

- **Will Paterson**
  willpaterson.design

- **Dean Rodriguez**
  lettershoppe.com

- **Pentagram**
  pentagram.com

- **Moving Brands**
  movingbrands.com

- **Landor&Fitch**
  landorandfitch.com

- **Wolff Olins**
  wolffolins.com

- **House Industries**
  houseindustries.com

- **Collins**
  wearecollins.com

- **SomeOne**
  someoneinlondon.com

- **Paul Rand (1914-1996)**
  paulrand.design

- **Saul Bass (1920 - 1996)**

- **Herb Lubalin (1918 - 1981)**

TRADEMARK PROTECTION

One company that I want to draw your attention to is **Trade Mark Wizards**, which is based in the UK.

I've been collaborating with the founder, Oliver Oguz, for several years and he's always provided superb service to me and my clients. If you have questions about trademark protection or are looking for an attorney to help protect the logos you design, I highly recommend *Trade Mark Wizards*.

trademarkwizards.co.uk

DESIGN PODCASTS

There are many superb design podcasts out there (aside from *The Logo Geek Podcast*) that I can recommend. Here are a few that I'm subscribed to, actively listen to and enjoy:

- **Honest Designer's Show.** Truly honest and practical advice from the founder of Design Cuts, Tom Ross, who hosts the show along with Ian Barnard, Dustin Lee and Lisa Glanz.
  logogeek.uk/honest-designers

- **Resourceful Designer.** A podcast hosted by Mark Des Cotes, aimed at home-based freelance designers, offering tips, tricks, advice and resources.
  logogeek.uk/resourceful-designer

- **The Futur Podcast.** Chris Do is one of the design industry's treasures, and his podcast is always a joy to listen to. He has a calming voice, asks challenging questions, and manages to uncover the best advice and insights from his superb guests.
logogeek.uk/the-futur-podcast

- **Obsessed Show.** Show host Josh Miles interviews some of the biggest names, from branding and illustration to industrial design and architecture.
logogeek.uk/obsessed-show

- **Design Matters.** In 2005, Debbie Millman started a radio show, which became the first-ever podcast about design. She's interviewed some of the greatest minds in design and dives deep into creative culture.
logogeek.uk/design-matters

- **The Design of Business | The Business of Design.** A podcast from Jessica Helfand and Pentagram co-founder Michael Bierut who interview creative visionaries for a deep dive discussion.
logogeek.uk/design-of-business

- **Design Life.** A podcast about design and side projects for motivated creators. Hosted by the amazing Charli Prangley and Femke van Schoonhoven.
logogeek.uk/design-life

- **See Through Design.** A relatively new podcast created by two good friends, Caz Cusumano and Liam Jackson. They have honest and open conversations around design that are a joy to listen to.
logogeek.uk/see-through-design

BRAND STRATEGY

BRAND EXPERTS

Brand Strategy is a vast topic, with many frameworks and tools available to help solve business problems. This book barely scrapes the surface of the topic, and since logo design is so deeply rooted in brand strategy, it's worth diving into the subject further by following and learning from experts. Here are a few I personally follow:

- **Marty Neumeier**
  martyneumeier.com

- **Fabian Geyrhalter**
  finien.com

- **Douglas Davies**
  douglasdavis.com

- **Matt Davies**
  mrmattdavies.me

- **Philip VanDusen**
  philipvandusen.com

- **Chris Do**
  thefutur.com

- **Melinda Livesey**
  melindalivsey.com

- **Stephen Houraghan**
  brandmasteracademy.com

USEFUL NAMING RESOURCES

Naming stuff is hard. Not because it's challenging to come up with ideas, but difficult because you need to find a name that's original, relevant and protectable.

If this is a service you're keen to offer clients along with logo design, which I've personally done, here's a list of valuable resources I've come across to help with the challenge of naming companies:

- **Onym Resources.** A deep rabbit hole of the best tools and resources for naming things.
  logogeek.uk/naming1

- **Don't Call It That: A Naming Workbook.**
  by Eli Altman.
  logogeek.uk/naming2

- **Namech_k.** A handy website to check the availability of usernames and domain names within seconds.
  logogeek.uk/naming3

- **A 3-step process for naming a project/product.**
  A superb blog by Ben Pieratt, with a long list of resources too.
  logogeek.uk/naming4

- **The Ultimate Guide: How to Come Up With a Business Name.** A blog by Grant Polachek.
  logogeek.uk/naming5

MARKETING

Marketing is a deep rabbit hole. While my focus has been design, throughout my career, there have been a handful of experts and blogs I've followed, learned from, and recommend checking out.

MARKETING & SEO EXPERTS

- **Pat Flynn.** I honestly love this guy and learned so much from him. He shares everything he knows and brings on the biggest and best experts to dive deeper into marketing and business topics. If you're into building a passive income alongside logo design, this is the guy to follow.
patflynn.com

- **Chris Ducker.** I came across Chris through his friendship with Pat, and it led me to discover the incredible YouPrenuer Summit, an entrepreneurial event that happened in London. He's the author of Rise of the YouPrenuer, a book that covers everything you need to know to build a thriving business around "you." He shares valuable insights through blogs, podcasts, videos, tutorials, and more, all created to help you build a profitable personal brand.
chrisducker.com

- **Neil Patel.** An oracle of information related to SEO and various aspects of online marketing.
neilpatel.com

- **Ryan Robinson.** A friend that's been hugely successful teaching others how to build a profitable blog. A big part of this involves SEO, and I am very confident he knows his stuff and is someone worth listening to. ryrob.com

- **Amy Porterfield.** Host of the Online Marketing Made Easy podcast and founder of a personal brand that's earned more than $82 million in revenue. She's someone worth following. amyporterfield.com

- **Grant Cardone.** A world-renowned entrepreneur, author, speaker, investor, and coach. Everything he does focuses on 10X Your Business and Income, which are lessons you can apply to your business. grantcardone.com

- **Gary Vaynerchuk.** A serial entrepreneur who's a content-producing machine with cameras following his every move. He churns out podcasts, videos, and books, is frequently a headline speaker, and is one of the biggest names in marketing. garyvaynerchuk.com

MARKETING & SEO BLOGS

- **Smart passive income.** A blog and podcast from Pat Flynn that dives into every aspect of business, including online marketing and SEO. smartpassiveincome.com

- **Semrush.** An online visibility management and content marketing platform with a great blog that will take you through the basics of SEO and dive deeper into related topics.
  semrush.com/blog

- **Search Engine Land.** A blog that goes deep into all aspects of digital marketing, advertising and SEO.
  searchengineland.com

- **Ahrefs.** Known for its SEO tools and resources to grow search traffic. They have a great blog too.
  ahrefs.com/blog

- **Backlinko.** This a goldmine of information to help you learn more about backlinking, a crucial part of SEO.
  backlinko.com/blog

SOCIAL MEDIA POSTING TOOLS

- **Buffer.** Manage your social accounts from a single platform, where you can schedule posts and measure their performance.
  logogeek.uk/buffer

- **Hootsuite.** A social media management software designed to help you create engaging content and grow followers.
  logogeek.uk/hootsuite

- **Meet Edgar.** A social media tool that automatically pulls posts from your content library to keep your social posts fresh every day, on repeat.
  logogeek.uk/meetedgar

WORDPRESS THEMES & PLUGINS

- **Theme Forest.** While plenty of free WordPress themes are out there, I recommend buying a well-designed theme if you plan to take this route. Theme Forest offers a vast collection of options to choose from.
  logogeek.uk/themeforest

- **Semplice.** One of the best WordPress-based portfolio themes out there. Actually, it's a little more than a theme. It completely transforms the WordPress interface into a dedicated platform for building a beautiful portfolio website.
  logogeek.uk/semplice

- **Elementor.** A plugin that allows WordPress users to create and edit websites with a responsive drag-and-drop interface.
  logogeek.uk/elementor

- **SEO Yoast.** A plugin that enhances the SEO features available within WordPress.
  logogeek.uk/seo-yoast

- **Link Whisper.** Powered by AI, this WordPress plugin suggests relevant internal links when you start writing your content within the WordPress editor.
  logogeek.uk/link-whisper

- **Pretty Links.** A WordPress plugin that allows you to create shorter URLs and track their usage. It's how I've made all the links in this section of the book.
  logogeek.uk/pretty-links

- **WP Rocket.** A WordPress plugin that helps speed up your website's loading time, making it a better experience for visitors, and it also helps with SEO. logogeek.uk/wp-rocket

- **Cloudflare.** A global network designed to make your website more secure, faster, and reliable. While this isn't specific to WordPress, it's worth using to improve your website page speed. logogeek.uk/cloudflare

WEBFLOW TOOLS

One of the best things about WebFlow is that their website has a range of excellent (and enjoyable) tutorials to learn the tools thoroughly.

However, if you do want to learn more from someone outside of the organisation, who's designing with Webflow day to day, I recommend content by Ran Segall, who runs **Flux Academy**. His free content on YouTube is excellent, but if you're keen to deep dive with him, check out his Webflow Masterclass.

logogeek.uk/webflow-masterclass

WEBSITE DOMAINS & HOSTING

When building a website to promote your services, you'll need to purchase a website domain, and if using a platform like WordPress, you'll need hosting too. Here are a few companies I've used and am happy to recommend:

- **Bluehost**
  logogeek.uk/bluehost

- **123 Reg**
  logogeek.uk/123-reg

- **IONOS**
  logogeek.uk/ionos

- **Go Daddy**
  logogeek.uk/godaddy

BUSINESS STUFF

CONTRACTS & PROPOSALS

Having a contract in place when working with clients is crucial to clearly outline any agreed-upon terms and conditions and address potential issues. To help you get started, here is a list of helpful templates I've encountered:

AIGA Standard Form of Agreement for Design Services
logogeek.uk/contract1

- **Contract Killer.** A plain language contract template.
  logogeek.uk/contract2

- **Logo Design Client Proposal Template** by
  Smithographic.
  logogeek.uk/contract3

- **Contract Mint.** A collection of freelance
  contract templates.
  logogeek.uk/contract4

- **The Perfect Proposal.** Created by the Futur, it's
  everything you need to craft winning proposals:
  backed by decades of experience and millions of
  dollars in closed business. I've personally used this
  and found it extremely helpful.
  logogeek.uk/contract5

- **The Legal Kit.** Created by the Futur, this product
  shares contract templates based on what they've used
  for their design business in the US.
  logogeek.uk/contract6

- **The Ultimate Freelance, Course 03: Proposals and
  Contracts.** As part of Michael Janda's course, the
  third part is dedicated to proposals and contracts with
  templates included. Worth the money if you want to
  also watch someone talk through everything in detail.
  logogeek.uk/contract7

ACCOUNTING SOFTWARE

When working with clients, you'll want to create professional invoices and keep track of your profits and expenses. To do this properly, I recommend using an accounting software. Here are a few that I've used:

- **Xero**
  logogeek.uk/xero

- **FreshBooks**
  logogeek.uk/freshbooks

- **FreeAgent**
  logogeek.uk/freeagent

PRODUCTIVITY TOOLS

- **ChatGPT.** An incredible AI tool that can answer questions, generate text, and perform various tasks. It can help write blogs, plan topics, and write social posts… The possibilities are endless.
  logogeek.uk/chatgpt

- **Trello.** A useful web-based project management tool that helps you organise and prioritise tasks and projects.
  logogeek.uk/trello

- **Go Fucking Work.** Excuse the name! This is a Chrome extension that blocks unproductive sites and shares hilarious, motivational messages instead, so you can focus on what you should be doing.
  gofuckingwork.com

THE
END

...OF THIS BOOK, AND **THE START OF YOUR STORY.** I LOOK FORWARD TO DISCOVERING YOUR ADVENTURE ON A FUTURE EPISODE OF THE LOGO GEEK PODCAST. **GOOD LUCK!**

THANK YOU 💜

Bringing this book to life has been an incredible journey.

After I finished writing, I chose to launch the book through Kickstarter to offer friends, followers, and myself a deluxe edition. Since then, I've distributed it globally via print-on-demand, which is how you have this version in your hands.

The Kickstarter campaign was a phenomenal success, reaching nearly 1000% of its funding goal! I never anticipated such overwhelming support. My heartfelt thanks go out to the 272 backers who made this dream a reality.

A special shoutout goes to these amazing people who went above and beyond with their generous support:

- **Lee Matthew Jackson**: Host of Trailblazer FM, a podcast aimed at web agency owners looking to grow their business and achieve a better work-life balance. Check out his podcast here: trailblazer.fm and his personal website here: leematthewjackson.com. Lee was a big supporter of the book from the outset, not only financially but also kindly inviting me as a guest on his podcast, helping me reach more people and share my story. Thank you, Lee.

- **Mark Des Cotes:** Host of the Resourceful Designer Podcast. Mark supported my journey long before I even had a podcast, so he knows how much I've wanted to create this book and how hard I've worked to bring it to life. I'm extremely grateful for his support for the book, bringing me as a guest on his podcast, and frequently giving shoutouts and recommendations throughout the campaign. Go check out his podcast – it's one of my favourites: resourcefuldesigner.com.

- **Morten Rongaard**: Famously known as FatViking, the CEO and co-founder of Reality+, a Web3 gaming company. He's a pioneer in the field of Blockchain, Crypto, and everything Metaverse. I know Morten through Doctor Who Worlds Apart, a digital card game that I enjoy. So, I greatly appreciate his contribution, helping me get closer to my 1000% goal! Check out everything he and the team are doing here: realityplus.com.

- **Sharif El-Komi**: A super talented designer based in Cairo, Egypt. I first met Sharif when he was featured as part of Chris Do's very first Futur Young Guns series. He's a young talent doing great things, and I'm proud to call him a friend. Thank you so much for the support Sharif! Make sure to check out his studios portfolio here: komi.studio.

In addition to the above, I also want to give a big thank you to the amazing people who kindly offered to promote and support the book.

- First of all, a special thank you to **Bill Gardner** and **Ellen Mosiman** of Logo Lounge. After reaching out to Bill, he greeted me with open arms, like family. We had a wonderful Zoom call where he offered to do all he could to help promote the book and even did a few magic tricks for my daughter! With very little notice, Ellen organised an email blast, social posts, and a blog post too, all despite a busy schedule. It was more than I ever imagined, so thank you. I'm extremely grateful.

- Another shoutout goes to my friend and fellow logo designer, **James Martin**, who, being the gentleman he is, reached out and offered help to promote the Kickstarter campaign. James is one of the nicest, most genuine, and talented designers in this space, so I'm immensely grateful he shared this book with his massive Instagram audience, helping more designers discover the book. Honestly, James, it's appreciated.

I was also invited by amazing friends to be on their podcasts and blogs to discuss the book and help support the Kickstarter. In no particular order, this included: **Phillip Van Dusen**, **Chris Green**, **Arcui Usoara**, **Col Grey**, **Chris Do**, **Bob Gentle**, **Jaychrist Teves**, and **Michael Bruny-Groth**. Thank you all for the support and encouragement. I'm more grateful than you realise.

And a special final thank you, a big hug, and lots of love go to three important people.

- **Hayley Paget**, my sister, who kindly offered to read through the book, proofread, and provide honest feedback. It's no small feat to go through over 50,000 words, so I'm forever grateful for your feedback, support, and encouragement… even if you did draw butt sketches all over the book! (I used the word "but" too often, so on every page where it said "but" 3 times, she drew a butt; but, that's now fixed)

- **Jason Frostholm**, a friend, fellow designer, and Design Educator, who kindly reached out to read through the book and offer constructive feedback. He's been incredibly supportive throughout, which took weeks of work, so Jason… I can't thank you enough. I hope one day I can return the favour.

- The most special thank you goes to my precious daughter **Evie Rose Paget**, who has given me the motivation to finish this book. Although just 4 years old at the time of writing this, she's been very involved in the book's promotion, helping to create fun little videos that make me, friends, and supporters laugh and smile with her cheeky comments! I love you more than anything, Evie, and I hope this book will show you that hard work pays off. Don't wait for opportunities to come your way... make them happen instead.

And finally, thank you to **YOU**, reading now. This book has been a dream to write for most of my adult life, and while it's one of the hardest things I've done, it's also been one of the most fulfilling. Thank you for trusting me, for supporting the book, and for reading it too. I genuinely hope it helps support your goals... Remember to dream big and do everything in your power to make those dreams a reality... don't chase money... chase those dreams... chase fulfilment... chase happiness! That's all that matters.

If you enjoyed this book, please take a photo of yourself with the book, share it on social media, and tag me, @logogeek – it brings such joy to see that people found the book useful, making the hard work and effort creating it worth it. Seriously, thank you.